All-in-One Sunday School

Volume 4

Summer

by Lois Keffer

Group

Loveland, Colorado
group.com

Dedication

To Bob—first, last, and always.

All-in-One Sunday School

Volume 4
Copyright © 1992, 2011 Lois Keffer

Visit our website: **group.com**

Credits
Author: Lois Keffer
Cover Design: RoseAnne Sather
Interior Design: Jan Fonda and Suzi Jensen
Illustrations: Matt Wood

ISBN 978-0-7644-4947-5
Printed in the United States of America.
10 9 8 7 6 5   14 13 12

TABLE OF CONTENTS

THE LESSONS

INTRODUCTION

Dear friend in children's ministry,

It's summer—hurray! We open this quarter with a bang—four lessons on the armor of God. Then comes a Sunday for a patriotic celebration, followed by all-important lessons on spiritual disciplines, the building-blocks of a mature faith. It's an action-packed summer you and your kids won't want to miss!

Like you, I have always been drawn to kids, and they to me. They pick me out in grocery store lines, on busy sidewalks and from passing cars. I think it's because they recognize someone who's never grown up! My teaching never became very "adult"—oh, no! Why? Because I saw the look of boredom that came over kids' faces when they sat down with the same ole' workbooks at Sunday school that they were used to year after year.

But when Sunday school involved active challenges, storytelling and play that were melded into learning experiences with carefully crafted questions to help kids tie Scriptural truth into their own lives—WOW! ZINGO! ZAP!—the learning lights went on! Discipline problems melted away. In our small church, grade school kids of all ages learned together.

Before we knew it, the adults wanted some of what the kids were getting, so we scheduled special intergenerational Sundays when the walls came down and the whole church learned together. And that's how *Sunday School Specials* was born, almost 20 years ago.

At that time, we had no idea that one little book of lessons would turn into a series of four, or that the four would continue to find favor in the marketplace for years and years. Thank you who have faithfully bought these books! And bless God who continues to surprise us!

So here's our new format: updated content, a fresh face, and year-long scope and sequence to turn the four *Sunday School Specials* books into *All-In-One Sunday School*. Book 1 begins with September quarter, Books 2, 3 and 4 continue with December, March and June quarters respectively. So your favorite *Sunday School Specials* lessons plus a few totally new and some updated ones now form a through-the-year curriculum for you and your kids to enjoy together. Just so the adults don't feel left out, we've noted certain lessons that would be appropriate for intergenerational learning.

If you have a smaller Sunday school, are cramped for space or short on teachers, *All-In-One Sunday School* is just what you need to keep lively Bible learning going in your church without stretching your resources. Teachers can volunteer week by week, month by month, or in whatever pattern works best for you. Best of all, you can combine your grade-school kids and be assured that everyone will get the most out of each week's lesson to apply foundational Bible truths to their lives.

I'm so excited to make this resource available to you. I hope you'll love it as much as I've loved working on it!

Lois Keffer

ACTIVE LEARNING IN COMBINED CLASSES

Research shows people remember most of what they do but only a small percentage of what they hear—which means kids don't do their best learning sitting around a table talking! They need to be involved in lively activities that help bring home the truth of the lesson. Active learning involves teaching through experiences.

Children do things that help them understand important principles, messages, and ideas. Active learning is a discovery process that helps them internalize the truth as it unfolds. Kids don't sit and listen as a teacher tells them what to think and believe—they find out for themselves. Teachers also learn in the process!

Each active-learning experience is followed by questions that encourage kids to share their feelings about what just happened. Further discussion questions help kids interpret their feelings and decide how this truth affects their lives. The final part of each lesson challenges kids to decide what they'll do with what they've learned—how they'll apply it to their lives during the coming week.

How do kids feel about active learning? They love it! Sunday school becomes exciting, slightly unpredictable, and more relevant and life-changing than ever before. So put the table aside, gather your props, and prepare for some unique and memorable learning experiences!

Active learning works beautifully in combined classes. When the group is playing a game or acting out a Bible story, kids of all ages can participate on an equal level. You don't need to worry about reading levels and writing skills. Everyone gets a chance to make important contributions to class activities and discussions.

These simple classroom tips will help you get your combined class off to a smooth start:

♦ When kids form groups, aim for an equal balance of older and younger kids in each group. Encourage the older kids to act as coaches to help younger ones get in the swing of each activity.

♦ In "pair-share," everyone works with a partner. When it's time to report to the whole group, each person tells his or her partner's response. This simple technique teaches kids to listen and to cooperate with each other.

♦ If an activity calls for reading or writing, pair young non-readers with older kids who can lend their skills. Older kids enjoy the esteem-boost that comes with acting as a mentor, and younger kids appreciate getting special attention and broadening their skills.

♦ Don't worry too much about discussion going over the heads of younger children. They'll be stimulated by what they hear the older kids saying. You may be surprised to find some of the most insightful discussion literally coming "out of the mouths of babes."

♦ Make it a point to give everyone—not just those who are academically or athletically gifted—a chance to shine. Affirm kids for their cooperative attitudes when you see them working well together and encouraging each other.

♦ Keep in mind kids may give unexpected answers. That's okay. The answers given in parentheses after questions are simply suggestions of what kids *may* say, not the "right" answers. When kids give "wrong" answers, don't correct them. Say something like: "That's interesting. Let's look at it from another viewpoint." Then ask for ideas from other kids. If you correct their answers, most kids will soon stop offering them.

HOW TO GET STARTED WITH ALL-IN-ONE SUNDAY SCHOOL

Teaching Staff

When you combine Sunday school classes, teachers get a break! Teachers who would normally be teaching in your 4- to 12-year-old age groups may want to take turns. Or ask teachers to sign up for the Sundays they'll be available to teach.

Lessons

The lessons in the *All-in-One Sunday School* series are grouped by quarter—fall, winter, spring, and summer—but each lesson can also stand on its own. Several of the lessons contain suggestions for using an intergenerational approach—inviting parents and other adults in the congregation to join the class. You may want to schedule these lessons for special Sundays in your church calendar.

Preparation

Each week you'll need to gather the easy-to-find props in the You'll Need section and photocopy the reproducible handouts. Add to that a careful read of the lesson and Scripture passages, and you're ready to go!

QUICK-GRAB ACTIVITIES

What do you do when kids arrive 15 minutes early? When one group finishes before others do? When there's extra time after class is over? Get kids involved in a Quick-Grab Activity!

How I'm Feeling Faces Board

Use newsprint or a white board or chalk board for this activity. Write "How I'm Feeling Faces" across the top. As kids arrive, invite them to draw a face that shows how they're feeling—happy, sad, mad, rushed, excited, upset, or lonely. The first time you use this activity, explain it to the kids and brainstorm different emotions they might express on the board. Ask them to initial the faces they draw.

Encourage kids to ask questions about each other's feelings. For instance, if someone draws a sad face, a friend might say, "I'm sorry to see you drew a sad face. Did you have a bad day at school?"

This can be a great tool for kids to use to learn to care for each other in deeper, more meaningful ways. You may also want to use it during guided prayer times with the children.

By the way, don't forget to draw your own "How I'm Feeling Face." Your participation will encourage the kids to participate as well. And if they discover that you've had a rough day, you'll be surprised at how extra thoughtful they will be!

Best or Worst Thing This Week Board

You guessed it—this works just the like the How I'm Feeling Faces Board. In fact, you make want to alternate the two. Invite kids to draw or write about their best or worst experiences of the week. This board may start off with superficial experiences, but it will soon grow to a depth that surprises you.

Kids really want to tell about themselves—to know and be known. One drawback of filling every minute of Sunday school is losing that intimate moment when a child would like to talk about a concern or unburden herself of a fear. A medium such as this lets kids form a pattern of sharing themselves in a nonthreatening way, which can lead to the sense of true community we all seek within God's family.

Prep and Takedown

If kids love your class—and they will!—they'll be more than willing to do everything that needs to be done to get going. So if you need chairs, handouts or supplies arranged, task your charming youngsters with the job. Have you noticed how a child's sense of worth soars when it is his particular responsibility to see that each person has a handout? Or when she gets to pack the teacher's bag?

Small jobs like these also create ownership in the class, which translates to less discipline issues. *Hey this is my class so I'm not going to mess it up!*

Whenever you say during class, "I need a helper, " you'll get a wind-farm's worth of waving arms. The same goes for before and after class as well! So put all that youthful enthusiasm to work and you'll have kids champing at the bit before class even begins.

Jabber Mat®

Group's Jabber Mat® is an on-the-floor, all-out-fun resource loaded with games and challenges for your class. Once you've used it, you'll wonder what you ever did without it! Purchase this instant go-to activity mat from Group Publishing (group.com/jabbermat).

LESSON

1

LESSON AIM

To help kids understand that ★ God offers us the free gift of salvation.

OBJECTIVES

Kids will

✓ play a game that involves unequal trades,
✓ hear what Jesus offered the dying thief,
✓ make paper "helmets of salvation," and
✓ have the opportunity to accept God's forgiveness and grace.

YOU'LL NEED

❏ small prizes or treats*
❏ small boxes or bags
❏ pennies
❏ miniature marshmallows*
❏ round toothpicks
❏ a CD player
❏ a CD of soft worship music
❏ photocopies of the "Helmet of Salvation" handout (p. 18)
❏ scissors
*Always check for allergies before serving snacks.

BIBLE BASIS

Ephesians 6:17

"That kid just doesn't have her head on straight." How often have you heard that expression? It usually indicates that the child in question is mentally or spiritually confused, displays wrong attitudes, and is otherwise generally discombobulated. As we "dress" our kids in the armor of God, let's work from the

all-in-one
SUNDAY
SCHOOL

top down. Let's begin with the helmet of salvation and teach kids how to get their heads on straight! They need to understand that accepting God's offer of salvation means that

♦ they're forgiven. Thanks to Christ's redemptive work on the cross, their sins are no more. They're new creatures.

♦ they choose to be on God's side and to give God their loyalty.

♦ they choose to follow Jesus and to live as he did—lives that exemplify love and grace.

♦ they become heirs to God's kingdom and a glorious future in heaven.

Use this lesson to teach kids that accepting God's free gift of salvation is the only qualification they need to receive all the other great benefits that go along with being God's children. It's their key to the locker where all the other pieces of armor are kept, their first step into life in the Spirit with all its wonderful fruit, and their ticket to eternity in heaven.

Each denomination has its own expectations about how the step of salvation should be taken. Take time during this lesson to explain your church's view of this all-important process.

Luke 23:26–24:7

No Scripture more graphically illustrates the "unfair" trade that God freely offers than this conversation between Jesus and the dying thief who believed in him. Could it be that God loves humankind so much that when a thief who lives a life of crime professes faith with his dying breath, God will receive him? God will cleanse his heart and give him eternity in heaven? Absolutely!

UNDERSTANDING YOUR KIDS

As you teach kids these basic tenets of the Christian faith, be prepared for all kinds of responses. Some kids may reflect spiritual understanding far beyond their years. Some may display a hunger for God and a strong realization of personal inadequacy. Others may just be taking their first steps down that path. It's not always the oldest and brightest who are the most spiritually mature. You're the guide, and you're assisted by none other than the Holy Spirit. Use this lesson to teach kids that to put on the helmet of salvation is to step into the light of God's grace.

The Lesson 😊

ATTENTION GRABBER

The Price Is Wrong

Before class, set out various small prizes on a table and hide each prize under a small box or a bag turned upside down. The prizes might include quarters, fancy pencils, erasers, or treats. You'll need one prize for each child, plus a couple of extras in case you have visitors. As kids enter, whet their curiosity about what might be hidden under the boxes and bags, but warn them that peeking disqualifies them from the game that's about to begin.

Have kids line up according to birthdays, the youngest in front and the oldest in back. Say: **We're going to begin today with a game. I'll give each of you a penny; then you'll have to decide if you want to keep the penny or trade it for one of the prizes on the table. If you decide to trade, you may choose one box or bag. There might be a good prize in the box or bag you choose, or there might be nothing at all.**

Hand the first child in line a penny and ask:

♦ **Would you rather keep your penny or have one of the prizes that's hidden on the table?**

If the child wants a prize, take the penny, and allow him or her to reveal one of the prizes on the table. The child must reveal only one prize, take the prize, and sit down. If the child prefers to keep the penny, simply have him or her sit down.

Repeat this process with each child. It will soon become obvious that all the prizes are worth much more than a penny. When everyone has played, gather kids in a circle and ask:

♦ **What did you think about this game?** (It was weird because the prizes were all worth more than the pennies; it was set up so we'd all want to trade our pennies for the prizes.)

♦ **Why do you think I'd set up a game where you all get better prizes than the pennies I gave you in the first place?** (Because you like us; because you wanted to make it fun; because that's what the book said to do.)

Say: **This game is called The Price Is Wrong because you all had a chance to trade for something much better than your pennies. Today we're going to find out how God offers us a trade that's even better than the trades I offered you in our game. We're going to learn that ★ God offers us the free gift of salvation.**

Have children eat their treats or set their prizes aside so they won't be a distraction during the rest of the class.

> **Teacher Tip**
>
> *If you use edible prizes, it's best to make all the prizes edible so that everyone has a treat to enjoy.*

BIBLE STUDY

The Sweet Gospel Story (Luke 23:26–24:7)

Say: **To begin today's Bible story, everyone needs to make a marshmallow man. I'll pass around a box of toothpicks and a bag of miniature marshmallows. Everyone take three toothpicks and five marshmallows. You may eat one of the marshmallows.** Pass around the toothpicks and marshmallows.

When everyone is ready, say: **Okay, let's make our marshmallow men together.** Demonstrate as you give the following instructions. **First, push a toothpick into a marshmallow. The marshmallow is a foot; the toothpick is a leg. Now make a second foot and leg. Hold the tops of the legs together and slide on two marshmallows—one for the body and one for the head. Now break your last toothpick in half and push the halves into the body to form arms. Great! Now you each have a marshmallow man. Set it on the floor in front of you, and sit on your hands.** Ask:

♦ **How do you feel about your marshmallow man? Do you like it or care for it at all?** (Yes, it's cute; no, I think it's dumb.)

♦ **Suppose I got really mean and walked around the circle and stepped on each person's marshmallow man. How would that make you feel?** (Angry; sad; I wouldn't want it to get spoiled.)

♦ **Suppose your marshmallow man suddenly came to life, walked up your arm, and poked you in the eye? How would you feel about it then?** (I'd be mad; I'd laugh; I'd punch it.)

Say: **You see, in some ways we're like our marshmallow men. God made us and he loves us and cares about us a lot—much more than we care for our marshmallow men. But we have an enemy—Satan. Sometimes Satan does mean things to us, like if I went around the circle and stomped on your marshmallow men. Satan always tries to get us to mess up and do wrong things. Sometimes we do. We may lie or cheat or steal or be disrespectful to our parents or even to God. Some of you said you wouldn't like it if your marshmallow men poked you in the eye and hurt you. God doesn't like it when we do things that are hurtful to him.** Ask:

♦ **What are some of the things we do that are hurtful to God?** (Use his name to swear; be mean and selfish; disobey the Ten Commandments.)

Say: **Our God is holy and perfect. When we sin and do things that are wrong, it's as though we are turning our backs toward God. Our sin separates us from our holy God. To show that, let's put our marshmallow men behind our backs.** Put your marshmallow man behind your back.

But God loves us and misses us all the time we are separated. So, to fix our broken relationship, God decided to give

us an incredible gift—a gift that is worth much more than anything we could ever trade. God gave us the gift of his Son, Jesus. Jesus was a human being like us. But Jesus was much more than we are. He was both God and man. So, just like God, Jesus was perfect. He was tempted by Satan, but he never did any of the mean or wrong things that we do. He lived on earth to show us how we should live. He taught that loving God and loving others are the most important things in life.

After Jesus had taught and preached and healed people for almost three years, he paid for our sins by giving his own life. Jesus loved us so much that he was willing to do anything to fix our relationship with God. He took the punishment that we earned.

Use extra toothpicks to make three crosses side by side on the floor in front of you to represent Jesus and the two men who were crucified with him.

Roman soldiers hung Jesus on a cross to die. Two other men were put on crosses beside Jesus. They were both criminals. One of the criminals taunted Jesus and made fun of him. "Aren't you the Christ?" he asked. "Save yourself and us!"

But the other thief couldn't believe his ears. He could see that Jesus was someone special. Listen to what he said. Read Luke 23:40-42 aloud. Say: **What a thing to ask! This man was a criminal under a death sentence. And now, just as he was dying, he wanted Jesus to forgive him.** Ask:

♦ **Wasn't that too much to ask? Explain.** (No, because Jesus loved him; yes, because he was a bad guy.)

♦ **What did Jesus do?** (Forgave him; listened to him.)

Say: **Jesus could tell that this thief had faith in him. So, even though this man had lived a life of sin, Jesus turned to him and said, "Today you will be with me in paradise." Whoa!** Ask:

♦ **Was that a fair trade? A life of sin, maybe one hour of being good, and then he gets to go to heaven?** (No, but Jesus did it anyway; yes, because the man believed in Jesus.)

Say: **Do you know that God is willing to make that trade with each one of us? That's right, ★ God offers us the free gift of salvation. When we say, "God, please forgive my sins and make me clean inside and let me become Jesus' follower and live in heaven someday," God answers, "Yes, I'll do that for you. My Son Jesus paid for your sins, so now you can be my child. I'll love you and watch over you and guide your life. And when you die, you'll come and live with me forever in heaven."** Ask:

♦ **What do you think about that trade—our sins for becoming God's child and living in heaven someday?**

14

♦ **How is that like The Price Is Wrong game that we played at the beginning of class?** (It's a very good trade for us!)

Say: **That trade—that gift God gives us—is called salvation. It's a gift that God hopes each of us will accept.**

Take time at this point to explain your church's teaching about receiving God's forgiveness and free gift of salvation.

LIFE APPLICATION

Marshmallow Meditation

Say: **Remember the marshmallow man and how he was set behind your back to remind you that sin is like turning our backs on God? Because Jesus died, we don't have to be separated from God. You can bring that marshmallow man back out and take a look at it. Because of Jesus' great gift, we can come face to face with God. We don't have to be separated from him. I'll play some soft music as you pray silently. You may want to thank Jesus for being willing to die for us, you may want to thank Jesus for taking the blame for your sins, or you may want to pray for forgiveness. Let's spend a few moments in silent prayer.**

Play soft worship music as kids pray silently. Then close by praying aloud: **Thank you, Lord, for taking our sins and offering us the free gift of salvation. In Jesus' name, amen.**

COMMITMENT

Salvation Helmets

Before class, make a sample "Helmet of Salvation" from the handout found at the end of this lesson.

Say: **When we accept God's free gift of salvation, we literally put on a piece of the armor of God—the helmet of salvation.** Ask:

♦ **What does a helmet do?** (Protects someone's head; acts as a second skull.)

♦ **What do you think the helmet of salvation might protect you from?**

Say: **Listen to what the Bible says about the whole armor of God and why we need it. See if you can identify how many pieces of armor there are.** Read aloud Ephesians 6:10-18. Then ask:

♦ **How many pieces of armor did you count?** (Six, plus prayer.)

♦ **What did you learn about why we need armor?** (Because we're on God's side in a battle between good and evil; because the evil one tries to hurt us.)

♦ **Why do you think the helmet of salvation is particularly important?** (Because it helps us think about good things; it reminds us of Jesus' love for us.)

Say: **God's armor protects us from our spiritual enemies.** Ask:

♦ **Who might not want us to be successful in our spiritual lives?** (Satan; people who are not on God's side.)

♦ **What might our spiritual enemies try to get us to do?** (Sin; disobey God.)

Say: **We Christians need to put on the helmet of salvation to protect ourselves. In upcoming lessons, we'll learn more about the full armor of God.** Put on the helmet of salvation you made before class. **These paper helmets can remind us of the real protection God's armor gives us.**

Distribute scissors and photocopies of the "Helmet of Salvation" handout. Explain that kids are to fold on the dotted lines and cut on the solid lines. Then they'll gently stretch the helmets over their heads.

When all the kids have put on their helmets, say: **These helmets identify us as people who are on God's side in all spiritual conflicts. Now repeat after me!** Lead this rhyme as if it were a marching cadence, with the kids repeating each line.

**I don't know, but I've been told
The armor of God makes me strong and *bold!***

**See the helmet of salvation on my head?
God took my sins and gave me heaven instead.**

Then ask:

♦ **Besides heaven, what are some other privileges we receive by accepting God's forgiveness?** (Talking to God face to face; protection from spiritual enemies.)

Continue the cadence as a prayer:

**Thank you, God, for these good gifts!
Help me live as you want me to live.**

CLOSING

Let the Helmet Speak

Ask:

♦ **What does it mean to you to put on the helmet of salvation?** (That I've accepted God's gift of forgiveness; that I'll live in heaven someday; that I'm a follower of Jesus; that I have eternal life.)

Say: **Good answers! Wearing the helmet of salvation also means that you are identified as a follower of Jesus, that he is your Lord and leader. Besides the helmet of salvation,** there are several other pieces of armor for God's people. You can read about them in the verses printed on your helmet.

Have kids take off their helmets. Ask volunteers to read each "ring" of the helmet aloud.

Say: **During upcoming lessons, we'll learn more about the other pieces of armor and how to put them on. If you enjoy memorizing, these are great verses to learn by heart. They'll help you remember all the protection you have as a person on God's side.**

Now I have an assignment I hope you'll accept. Show your helmet of salvation to someone this week, and explain what it reminds you of—that ★ God offers us the free gift of salvation.

Make sure kids take their marshmallow men and their helmets of salvation as they leave.

HELMET OF SALVATION

Cut out the circle, and fold it in half on one dotted line and in half again on the other dotted line.
Cut on the solid lines; then open the helmet, and gently stretch it over your head.

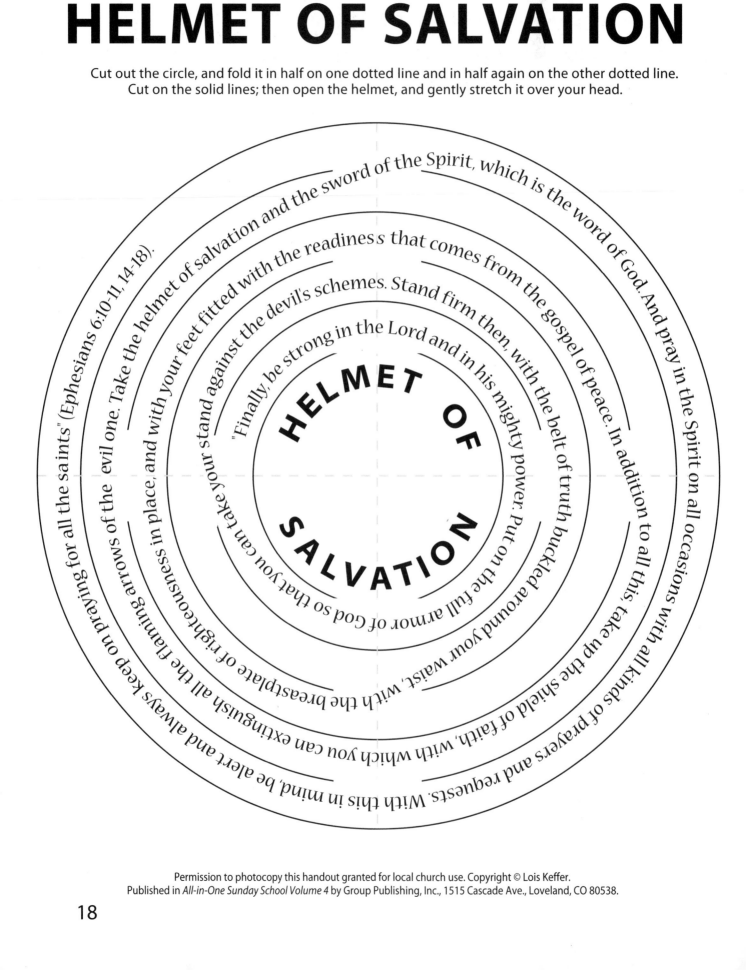

HELMET OF SALVATION

"Finally, be strong in the Lord and in his mighty power. Put on the full armor of God so that you can take your stand against the devil's schemes. Stand firm then, with the belt of truth buckled around your waist, with the breastplate of righteousness in place, and with your feet fitted with the readiness that comes from the gospel of peace. In addition to all this, take up the shield of faith, with which you can extinguish all the flaming arrows of the evil one. Take the helmet of salvation and the sword of the Spirit, which is the word of God. And pray in the Spirit on all occasions with all kinds of prayers and requests. With this in mind, be alert and always keep on praying for all the saints" (Ephesians 6:10-11, 14-18).

Breastplate, Belt, and Shield

LESSON AIM

To help kids understand that ★ God gives us his armor to protect us.

OBJECTIVES

Kids will

✓ play a game and try to knock each other off balance,
✓ learn how God protected Daniel,
✓ identify ways Satan might try to defeat them and how they can resist, and
✓ make a commitment to wear God's armor by being truthful, doing what's right, and having faith in God.

YOU'LL NEED

❏ a photocopy of the "Quietest Lions Around" story (pp. 23-24)
❏ office paper used on one side
❏ photocopies on card stock of the "Breastplate, Belt, and Shield" handout (p. 28)
❏ disposable aluminum pie pans
❏ scissors
❏ masking tape

BIBLE BASIS

Daniel 6:1-28

Daniel distinguished himself among King Darius' advisers and thus became the target of his peers' jealousy. Consumed with the desire to bring Daniel down, the other rulers conspired against him. But Daniel was so pure in heart and

all-in-one
SUNDAY
SCHOOL

actions that his detractors finally realized that they would never be able to discredit him unless they did it through cunning entrapment. So the snare was laid—they persuaded the king to sign into law a decree that for 30 days, no one should pray to anyone but the king. Violation of this decree would result in a one-way ticket to a den of hungry lions.

Now put yourself in Daniel's shoes. Would you have gone to your room to pray, as Jesus suggested hundreds of years later? Would you have at least gone inside your house? Not Daniel. He knelt to pray in the window of an upstairs room where he could face Jerusalem. And the villains arrested him. But for reasons yet unknown to Darius, the lions lost their appetite at the sight of this godly man, regaining it when Daniel's detractors were lowered into the den. God's mighty power was at work!

Ephesians 6:14, 16

Eph 6:13

It sometimes seems that the world is a minefield for those who commit themselves to living godly lives. For God's people today, the best offense is still a good defense. The breastplate of righteousness prevented Daniel's enemies from finding any fault in his dealings. Because the belt of truth was around him, scrupulous honesty made him invulnerable to criticism. And when conspirators shot the fiery arrows of deception and malice, the shield of faith protected Daniel from all harm.

UNDERSTANDING YOUR KIDS

Kids from godly families often "stick out" as much as Daniel did. "No, I haven't seen that horror movie." "Yes, I believe God created the world." "No, you can't copy my homework." "Yes, I believe people should wait until they're married to have sex." "No, I won't lie to cover up what happened." "Hey—leave the new kid alone. He may be different from the rest of us, but that's no reason to make fun of him." Kids soon learn that the world doesn't always take kindly to people who live according to a higher standard. Use this lesson to teach kids that when they identify themselves as God's people, they'll probably meet with opposition but God will surround them with his care.

ATTENTION GRABBER

A Real Pushover

Say: **Let's begin today with a game. Find a partner who is about as tall as you are. Stand facing that person. Your feet must be together, no more than 12 inches from your partner's feet. Now hold up your hands and press them against your partner's hands.** Check to make sure all the pairs are in the correct position. **When I say "go," you may start pushing against your partner's hands so that your partner loses his or her balance. You don't want to knock your partner over— your goal is to cause your partner to get off-balance enough to have to move his or her feet. If you both end up moving your feet at the same time, start over. No hitting or bumping—you may only push your hands against your partner's hands. Has everybody got it? Go!**

ALTERNATE GAME

Lead kids to a carpeted or grassy area. Say: **Please line up shoulder to shoulder.** Place yourself at one end of the line. **I'll do a motion; then the person next to me will do it and pass it down the line. Then I'll do another motion and pass it down the line. Keep on copying my actions, and stay close to the people beside you.**

Lead the kids in these actions:

♦ kneel on your left knee;

♦ cross your right foot in front of your left knee;

♦ point far to the left with your right hand;

♦ point far to the right with your left hand;

♦ touch your nose to the inside of your arm.

At this point everyone will be twisted up and crouched close to the ground. Gently push the shoulder of the person next to you, and the whole line of kids will tip over like dominoes. It's a very silly feeling and a funny sight! Because kids are already so close to the ground, they just tip over gently rather than falling hard.

Let everyone enjoy a good laugh; then gather kids in a circle and ask:

♦ **What was it like to suddenly tip over?** (Really funny; a little weird; surprising.)

♦ **Why was it so easy for me to tip you over?** (Because we were all twisted up; because we weren't expecting it.)

Continue with the last paragraph before the Bible Study.

The alernate game is lots of fun and also makes the point of the lesson beautifully. Play it only if you can take the kids to a carpeted or grassy area. And bear in mind these two simple precautions: (1) If you have a rough or hyperactive child, keep him or her next to you in line, and (2) arrange the line of children so you won't have any large children tipping in the direction of smaller children.

If you choose to use the alternate game, pick up the discussion with the "Say" section located just above the Bible Study.

After the first round, let kids find new partners and play again. Then say: **Go back to your original partners. We're going to play a little differently this time. Stand about two feet from your partner, and plant your feet wide apart. Press your hands together and try to push your partner off balance when I say "go." Ready? Go!**

Kids will discover that standing with their feet apart gives them much more control. They'll find it harder to push their partners off balance and easier to hold their own feet in place. If kids are enjoying the game, let them play it with two or three other partners. Then call time. Bring everyone together and ask:

♦ **Tell which way you prefer to play the game—with your feet together or apart?** (I liked it with my feet together because it was easier to make my partner lose her balance; I liked it with feet apart because I could keep my balance better.)

Say: **Sometimes in life we get knocked off balance. Things creep up on us and surprise us, or we feel overwhelmed by things that are stronger than we are. ★ God has ways of helping us stay on our feet when life tries to knock us down. He is stronger than anything we'll ever face. God gives us his armor to protect us. Let's see how the armor of God protected a famous Bible character.**

BIBLE STUDY

The Quietest Lions Around (Daniel 6:1-28)

Photocopy the "Quietest Lions Around" story. Before class, choose two students to be action leaders for the story. Let them read through the story and practice the actions given in italics.

Say: **Today we have two action leaders who are going to help with the story. As I read the story, I'd like you to** *listen* **to me,** *watch* **the action leaders, and** *do* **what they do. Got that? Let's go.**

If time allows, you may want to go through the story twice to make sure kids understand the plot. At the end of the story, have everyone give the action leaders a big round of applause. Ask:

♦ **Why did Daniel have enemies who wanted to hurt him?** (Because he was their boss; because they were jealous; because the king liked Daniel best.)

22

THE QUIETEST LIONS AROUND

1 Darius was crowned king at age sixty-two.
(Use hands to make a crown.)
I think that's old for a king, how 'bout you?
The king needed helpers to rule all the land,
So he looked for some wise men to lend him a hand.
(Strike a thoughtful pose.)

2 Darius chose helpers—a hundred and twenty.
(Count on your fingers.)
He thought a hundred and twenty was plenty!
Then he chose three men who would help him the most.
(Hold up three fingers.)
Daniel was named to the number one post.
(Hold up one finger.)

3 Daniel was glad to advise the new king.
(Fold arms, smile, and nod.)
With wisdom from God, he could solve anything!
(Point up; then point to head.)
So beside his window each morning and night,
Daniel prayed and asked God to help him do right.
(Fold hands and bow head.)

4 The king's other helpers were greedy, mean fellas.
(Make a mean, snarly face.)
Having Daniel in charge of things made them all jealous.
They waited for Daniel to do something wrong;
(Look at watch; then sigh and shake head.)
Never has anyone waited so long!

5 They stormed, and they stewed, and they thought night and day.
(Scowl and scratch head.)
They'd get Daniel in trouble—there must be a way!
They thought and they thought; then one said with a nod,
"Let's get him in trouble for praying to God!"
(Nod and shake finger.)

6 "We'll make a new law! Here's what it will say:
(Pretend to unroll and read a scroll.)
'People must pray to the king when they pray.'
We'll get him to sign with the seal of his ring.
(Point to ring finger.)
Not a word can be changed. Not a bit! Not a thing!"

7 King Darius was flattered to hear this new deal.
(Pat hair and smile.)
He gladly approved it with his royal seal.
(Press fist into opposite hand.)
He was, after all, supreme ruler and king
(Put hands on head like a crown.)
And could tell all his subjects to do anything.

8 As soon as King Darius signed the new law,
They went after Daniel, and here's what they saw:
(March angrily; shield eyes and look up.)
Daniel was in his house, down on his knees
(Kneel and fold hands.)
Praying to God, just as bold as you please!

(continued)

9 They dragged faithful Daniel off to the king
(Pretend to pull someone.)
And said, "He's been doing a terrible thing—
(Point and stomp foot.)
Praying to God! Now don't you forget—
The law says he must be thrown in the pit."
(Point dramatically.)

10 There was no way that Darius could save his adviser.
(Shake head sadly.)
He said sadly, "Daniel, I should have been wiser!
I shouldn't have listened to those evil men;
(Put hands over ears.)
May your God protect you in that lions' den!"
(Point upward; clasp hands together.)

11 The king woke the next morning and jumped out of bed,
(Open eyes wide.)
Threw his robe 'round his shoulders, his crown on his head.
(Pretend to put on robe and crown.)
He pushed open the doors and flew from his room.
(Run in place.)
He had to find out what had happened—and soon!

12 As fast as he could, the king ran to the den,
(Continue to run in place.)
Sure that the lions had eaten his friend.
He stopped, looked, and listened, but heard not a sound.
(Cup hand around ear; shake head.)
Those cats were the quietest lions around!

13 "Daniel!" he called, "Did the God that you serve
(Cup hands around mouth.)
Keep you from being the lions' hors d'oeuvre?"
"Yes," Daniel answered. "I prayed through the night,
(Nod head and fold hands.)
And an angel shut all of the lions' mouths tight!"
(Put hands over mouth.)

14 "The great God I worship would never desert me;
(Raise hands and look up.)
Not once did those big, hungry cats try to hurt me.
(Cross arms and shake head.)
Not a growl did I hear, not a purr, not a roar,
(Cup hand around ear.)
Not a peep, not a sneeze, not a sniff, not a snore."

15 The king was delighted, and he gave a great shout,
(Raise fists in victory.)
"Come here, all you servants, and pull Daniel out!"
(Beckon; pretend to pull up on a rope.)
To all of the bad guys he said, "This is it.
Now it's your turn to go down into the pit!"
(Point forward; point down.)

16 Darius made up a new law right away;
(Pretend to read from a scroll.)
"Respect Daniel's God—he saved Daniel today!"
Then to the whole kingdom, they told Daniel's story,
(Spread arms wide.)
Worshipped the true God, and gave him great glory!
(Raise arms and look up.)

♦ **Why did it take Daniel's enemies so long to bring him down?** (Because he was good and honest; because he never did anything wrong.)

Say: **Daniel had put on the armor of God (even though it wasn't written about until hundreds of years later). God gives us his armor to protect us. One piece of armor is called the belt of truth.**

Ask:

♦ **What evidence do you see that Daniel was wearing the belt of truth?** (He didn't lie to get out of trouble; he didn't hide his praying.)

Say: **Another piece of God's armor is called the breastplate of righteousness. A breastplate is one of the largest and most important pieces of armor. It covered a soldier from his neck to his waist. Righteousness is living a life that is pleasing to God.** Ask:

♦ **What evidence do you see that Daniel was wearing the breastplate of righteousness?** (He followed God; no one would believe anything bad about him; everyone knew he always did the right thing.)

Say: **Daniel was good, honest, and godly, so his enemies couldn't find anything wrong with him. The only way they could hurt him was to make up a bad law.** Ask:

♦ **How did the bad law get Daniel in trouble?** (He prayed to God even when the law said he had to pray to the king.)

Say: **Even though the bad guys managed to pass a bad law, the shield of faith protected Daniel.** Ask:

♦ **What evidence do you see that Daniel was holding the shield of faith?** (He asked God for help; he prayed even though he knew he could be punished.)

Say: **Did you ever hear of hungry lions suddenly deciding that they're not so hungry after all? Daniel had faith in God, and God protected him so that everyone would know how mighty he is! The good news is that ★ God still gives us his armor to protect us. Let's find out how.**

LIFE APPLICATION

Shields Up!

Have each child take scissors, a pie pan, and a photocopy of the "Breastplate, Belt, and Shield" handout. As kids cut around the shield on the handout, distribute three 2-inch strips of masking tape to each child. Let kids fold the tape into rolls and use it to attach their shields to the bottoms of their pie pans. Explain that kids can hold their shields by the edges.

Then say: **I wonder if you know how to put on these pieces of armor.**

Ask:

♦ **How would you put on the belt of truth?** (By asking God to help you be honest; by always telling the truth.)

♦ **How would you put on the breastplate of righteousness?** (By asking God to help you do what's right; by asking God to forgive your sins; by trying to do what's right.)

♦ **How would you put on the shield of faith?** (By trusting God; by praying for God's help; by remembering that God is stronger than anyone or anything.)

Have kids form two groups. Give each group a stack of office paper that's been used on one side. Say: **Let's see how the armor of God protects us. The Bible tells us that the shield of faith can protect us from the flaming arrows of the evil one. In your groups, brainstorm how these pieces of armor might protect you from a particular temptation. For example, you might be tempted to lie about finishing your homework—someone wearing the belt of truth would risk taking a zero rather than lie. Each time your group names a temptation, crumple a sheet of paper into a wad. I'll give you two minutes to brainstorm and make paper wads.**

Visit both groups as they brainstorm, providing encouragement and ideas. Call time after two minutes. Lay a masking tape line down the middle of the room, and assign each group to one side of the line.

Say: **Let's see how your armor works. These paper wads represent flaming arrows of temptation. Group 1, you'll throw your paper wads at Group 2, and Group 2 will use its shields to block them. Is everybody ready? Go!**

After kids in Group 1 have thrown all their paper wads, have the groups switch roles so Group 2 throws and Group 1 blocks with its shields. When all the paper wads have been thrown, give half the paper wads back to Group 1.

Say: **Now you can throw and block at the same time. Throw any paper wad that's near you as you use your shields to block paper wads that come your way. When I clap three times, that's your signal to stop.**

Let kids play for a minute or two; then call time by clapping your hands. Have kids pile the paper wads in one corner of the room and then sit in a circle.

Ask:

♦ **How well did you protect yourself?** (Pretty well; OK.)

♦ **How does God's armor compare to the little shield you used to defend yourself?** (It's stronger because God is stronger than anyone; God's armor works better.)

COMMITMENT

Armor Rap

♦ **How can you put on God's armor each day?** (I can pray; I can ask God to be with me.)

Say: **It's important to remember that** ★ **God gives us his armor to protect us. Let's learn three more verses of the "Armor of God Rap" that we started to learn last week.** Review the verses that kids learned last week by having them repeat after you in a marching cadence rhythm. Then add the three new verses.

I don't know, but I've been told
The armor of God makes me strong and *bold!*

See the helmet of salvation on my head?
God took my sins and gave me heaven instead.

Is the breastplate of righteousness on my chest?
Uh-huh! You can see that I'm wearin' God's best.

Is the belt of truth tied around my waist?
Uh-huh! I'm wrapped up in God's grace.

Is the shield of faith strapped on my arm?
Uh-huh! Satan's arrows will do me no harm.

Thank you, God, for these good gifts!
Help me live as you want me to live.

CLOSING

Armored Prayer

Say: **Good job! You'll find the new verses to the rap on your shield. See if you can learn them this week. Now form a tight circle around me. Face outward, and hold out your shield as I pray for all of us.**

Pray: **Dear Lord, thank you for** ★ **giving us your armor to protect us and help us stand strong. Help us to be truthful, to do what's right, and to have faith in you. Please protect each person here from all of Satan's attacks, and help us grow in our faith. In Jesus' name, amen.**

Be sure kids take their shields as they leave.

BREASTPLATE, BELT, AND SHIELD

Belt of Truth

Is the belt of truth tied around my waist?
Uh-huh! I am wrapped up in God's grace.

Breastplate of Righteousness

Is the breastplate of righteousness
on my chest?
Uh-huh! You can see that I'm
wearin' God's best.

Shield of Faith

Is the shield of faith strapped on my arm?
Uh-huh! Satan's arrows will do me no harm.

Prayer of Thanks

Thank you, God, for these good gifts!
Help me live as you want me to live.

LESSON AIM

To help kids understand that ★ God wants us to spread the good news.

OBJECTIVES

Kids will

✓ find hidden objects that tell about the life of Jesus,
✓ hear how Philip shared the good news,
✓ make Good News Shoes that tell the story of Jesus, and
✓ ask God to help them share the good news.

YOU'LL NEED

❑ straw or dried grass
❑ a small scrap of wood
❑ a sheep shape cut from white fleece or felt
❑ a Band-Aid
❑ a jewelry or paper heart
❑ a nail
❑ a small, round stone
❑ a small crown cut from foil
  Note: If you'd prefer not to gather the above items, you
    may use the pictures from the "Good News Scrolls"
    handout (p. 38) instead.
❑ 8 envelopes
❑ a photocopy of the "Philip's Visit" script (p. 33)
❑ a guest to play the role of Philip
❑ a costume for Philip—robe, sandals, fake beard, and
    mustache
❑ scissors
❑ photocopies of the "Good News Shoes" handout (p. 37)
❑ photocopies of the "Good News Scrolls" handout (p. 38)

all-in-one
SUNDAY
SCHOOL

BIBLE BASIS

Acts 8:26-40

Many people confuse the Philip of Acts 8 with Philip the apostle. Philip the apostle was a resident of Bethsaida; the Philip of Acts 8, also known as Philip the Evangelist (Acts 21:8), lived in Caesarea. He is first introduced in Acts 6:5 when he was chosen as one of the seven who were to oversee the daily distribution of food. Because of intense persecution in Jerusalem, Philip and many other Christians were forced to flee. Acts 8:4 tells us that "the believers who were scattered preached the good news about Jesus wherever they went." Philip went into a town in Samaria where he healed many people and drove out demons so that "there was great joy in that city" (verses 6-8).

The story of Philip and the Ethiopian eunuch certainly explains how Philip came to be known as "the Evangelist." An angel delivered Philip's marching orders to travel the road from Jerusalem to Gaza. On the road, Philip encountered an important Ethiopian official who just happened to be reading the book of Isaiah. When Philip ran alongside the chariot, the Ethiopian invited him to come up and explain the Scriptures. Before many miles had passed, the eunuch stopped the chariot so he could be baptized in acknowledgment of his newfound faith in Christ.

Even though we don't face the great perils that first century Christians encountered, somehow telling the good news has gotten to be bad news for too many Christians today. Why has sharing the gospel become a dreaded, onerous task? To put it simply, it is because we have an enemy whose flaming arrows fill us with doubt and cause us to shrink and hide. Will the person we're sharing with think we're weird? Will our little forays into really important issues earn us rejection or ridicule? Oh, if we could only step into Philip's shoes. What a runner he was—eager to speak of the wealth of God's love and the riches of becoming a child of God.

Ephesians 6:15

"You got shoes, I got shoes, all God's children got shoes…" Well, hallelujah! God wants us all to have shoes. Walkin', talkin' shoes. Shoes that carry us as we carry the good news of the gospel of peace. And it is *good news*. Through Christ, God offers to take our chaos, sin, and pain and give us peace in return. What a deal!

UNDERSTANDING YOUR KIDS

All God's children need shoes—and, boy, do they want brand names! The advertising doesn't get past them, that's for sure. If you've ever tried to get an elementary school child to settle for anything less, you're doubtless aware that such children invariably see your efforts to economize as the worst possible form of child abuse. Today, however, you can introduce your kids to a whole new category of elite shoes—shoes that transform the wearers into messengers for the King of heaven. Use this lesson to teach kids that, as exciting as it is to tie on those fancy new name-brand shoes, putting on the shoes that come with the armor of God is a much greater privilege—one that carries eternal significance.

The Lesson 😊

ATTENTION GRABBER

A Mystery Challenge

Before class, place the following items that relate to Jesus' life in separate envelopes: straw or dried grass (Jesus was born in a stable); a small scrap of wood (Jesus was a carpenter); a sheep shape cut from white fleece or felt using the pattern on page 38 (Jesus called himself the good shepherd); a Band-Aid (Jesus healed people); a jewelry or paper heart (Jesus taught us to love God and love others); a nail (Jesus took the punishment for our sins); a small, round stone (the stone was rolled away from Jesus' empty tomb); and a shiny foil crown made from the pattern on page 38 (Jesus reigns in heaven). Seal the envelopes, and hide them around the room.

When kids arrive, say: **The first thing you'll need to do today is solve a mystery. I'm not even going to tell you what the mystery is about. But I will tell you this: I've hidden several clues around the room. The clues are inside eight sealed envelopes. When I say "go," you may begin searching for the envelopes. Each person may find only one envelope. If you find one, don't open it. Just come back to our circle, and we'll open them together after they've all been found. Ready? Go!**

When kids have found all the envelopes, gather everyone in a circle. Call on kids who are holding the envelopes to open them one by one. Each time a child opens an envelope and reveals what's inside, ask:

♦ **What could this clue be about?**

Accept all suggestions, and don't give any particular direction to the discussion until all eight clues have been revealed. Then, if kids haven't already guessed, ask:

♦ **How do all eight of these clues tie together? What could they be about?**

♦ **How could all of these items relate to a single thing or person?**

Continue asking questions and dropping hints until kids discover that all the clues relate to the life of Jesus. Then say: **Good work! You guys are super detectives. Today we're going to talk about telling others about Jesus because ★ God wants us to spread the good news. Did you know that there's one piece of God's armor that's specifically meant to help us share the good news about Jesus? It's true. Let's meet a Bible character who wore that piece of armor and see how it helped him. On the count of three, let's call out, "Philip,**

Teacher Tip

If you're in a hurry to prepare the lesson, cut apart the pictures from the "Good News Scrolls" handout, and place the pictures in envelopes in place of the actual items. To make the search more fun, use brightly colored envelopes.

32

PHILIP'S VISIT

(based on Acts 6:1-6; 8:26-40)

(When you hear the kids call, "Philip, Philip, come on down," rush breathlessly into the room.)

Hi! Did you guys call me? I thought so. Well, it's nice to meet you. I'm Philip.

(Shake hands with a few of the kids, and ask their names.)

I guess you can see that I'm kind of out of breath. You wouldn't believe what just happened. Well, maybe you would believe it. After all, you're here in church, so you must know about the amazing things that God can do.

I've been working with Jesus' disciples for quite a while now. Not too long ago, the disciples chose seven men to help take care of church business in Jerusalem. They were so busy preaching and teaching that they needed other people to take care of poor people and do the everyday business of the church. I was one of seven who were chosen. Things got pretty hard in Jerusalem. We all shared our money and belongings, and that's how we took care of poor people. Then the Jewish leaders started making things hard for Christians in Jerusalem. Lots of our people were arrested and beaten—some were even put to death. So we had to scatter in all directions. But we pledged to preach the good news wherever we went.

Can any of you tell me what the good news about Jesus is?

(Let kids share their knowledge of the gospel.)

Hey, that's right! You guys are really on the ball. Good for you!

You know, people are really happy to hear about Jesus. Who wouldn't want to know that their sins can be forgiven and that they can become children of God and live in heaven someday? Talk about good news!

Well, back to my adventure. I was traveling through Samaria when suddenly an angel told me to walk down the road that goes to Gaza. So I did. And I saw a man who was an important government official in Ethiopia. He took care of the queen's money. Anyway, as he was riding along, he was reading the book of Isaiah. I started running alongside his chariot. "Do you understand what you're reading?" I asked him.

"How can I understand unless someone explains it to me?" he replied. Then he invited me to climb in and sit beside him. Whew—I was glad to accept. It's a little difficult to carry on a conversation when you're running!

Anyway, we talked, and I explained that Jesus died to take away the sins of the whole world and all we have to do is ask and Jesus will forgive our sins—then we can be children of God. This man was so happy to hear all this good news that he stopped his chariot by a stream and I baptized him right there. It was so exciting to see how much he loved God and how glad he was to have his sins forgiven!

Let me tell you, there's just nothing greater in this world than telling people about Jesus. And God wants us to spread the good news. I hope you'll share the good news every time you get the chance.

Well—I've got to run. There are lots more people like my Ethiopian friend who need to hear about Jesus. Thanks for inviting me to visit—I've had a great time. See ya!

(As you run from the room, turn and wave at the kids.)

Philip, come on down!"

Count to three, and lead kids in calling out to Philip.

BIBLE STUDY

The Gospel in Shoes (Acts 8:26-40)

Before class, arrange for a man to play the role of Philip and visit your class. Give him a photocopy of the script, "Philip's Visit." Have him wait outside your classroom until the kids call out, "Philip, Philip, come on down!" Or play Philip yourself. Quickly don a robe and sandals. If you're a woman, stick on a fake beard and mustache—the kids will love it.

Say: **Philip seemed really excited about telling people about Jesus.** Ask:

♦ **Why do you think he was he so excited?** (Because he helped a man become a Christian.)

♦ **Tell about a time you told someone about Jesus?** (I told my friend that Jesus would take care of him when his dad got sick; I invited my neighbor to vacation Bible school to hear about Jesus.)

♦ **Do you think telling people about Jesus is easy or hard? Explain.** (Hard, because people think you're weird; easy, because it's good news.)

Say: **The Bible tells us that it's important to tell people about Jesus whenever we can. Today we're going to learn how to do that. But we'll have to make sure that everyone has the right shoes on. Let me see your feet!** Inspect everyone's feet. **Nope—no one has the right shoes on. But never mind—I have shoes for you!**

LIFE APPLICATION

Good News Shoes

Distribute photocopies of the "Good News Shoes" handout. Say: **Believe it or not, these are shoes! They're Good News Shoes. They're part of the armor of God because ★ God wants us to spread the good news. Listen.**

Read Ephesians 6:14-15 aloud. Ask:

♦ **What do you think the Bible means by "put on the peace that comes from the good news so that you will be prepared"?** (We should be ready to tell people about Jesus; it's good news so we should feel peaceful about sharing it.)

Say: **"Prepared" is an important word here. It means that whenever we're talking with people who need to hear about Jesus, were ready to jump right in and tell them.**

Ask:

♦ **How do we know if people need to hear about Jesus?** (If they're sad or in trouble; if they've never heard about him.)

♦ **How did Philip find the Ethiopian man?** (An angel told him to go to that road; he heard the man reading from Isaiah.)

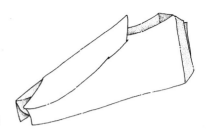

Say: **An angel of God told Philip to walk down that road, and Philip was on the lookout for someone he might help. We can be on the lookout, too. Every day we can pray, "Lord, if there's someone who needs to hear about you, please help me find that person today, and help me tell the good news." It's really that simple! And these Good News Shoes will help you know what to say and how to say it.**

Before class, use an X-Acto knife to open the three slits in the shoe patterns. Have kids cut out the shoes and fold up (valley folds) on all the dotted lines. Show them how to slip the tabs on the "tongue" of the shoe into the slits on the top and how to slip the tab at the back of the shoe into the slit at the back.

Then say: **Now you need something to put in your shoes.** Distribute the "Good News Scrolls" handout. Point out that the objects on the scrolls are similar to the objects kids found at the beginning of class. Let older kids take turns reading aloud the verses written beneath each object. After each verse is read, ask:

♦ **Using this picture and verse, what could you tell someone about Jesus?**

Here are suggested comments for each picture and verse.

1. Straw in a manger—God sent Jesus into the world as a tiny baby.
2. Wood—Jesus lived with his family and worked as a carpenter until he was about 30 years old.
3. Band-Aid—Then Jesus began traveling around, preaching, teaching, and healing people. Many people believed that he was the Messiah promised long ago.
4. Sheep—Jesus said that he was the good shepherd who loved his sheep and that he would lay down his life for his sheep.
5. Heart—Jesus taught that the most important thing is to love God and to love others. He taught that those who love him will show their love by obeying him.
6. Nail and cross—Jesus taught that everyone has sinned and needs to be forgiven. He died on the cross to take the punishment for the sins of the whole world.
7. Tomb with the stone rolled away—On the third day, Jesus came back to life.
8. Crown—If we believe in Jesus, we can live with him in heaven someday.

Then have kids cut out the two scrolls, roll them up, and slip them into their Good News Shoes.

COMMITMENT

Put Your Best Foot Forward

Say: **God wants us to spread the good news. Now that you have your Good News Shoes, you'll need to decide how to use them. Turn to a partner and tell about someone you might share your Good News Shoes with this week.**

After kids have shared, say: **It's time to rap and roll! Let's learn a new verse of the "Armor of God Rap."** Review the verses that kids learned last week by having them repeat after you in a marching cadence rhythm. Then add the new verse. For extra fun, make a human train by having kids line up and hold on to the waist of the next person in line. Lead the train around the room as you say the rap:

**I don't know, but I've been told
The armor of God makes me strong and *bold!***

**See the helmet of salvation on my head?
God took my sins and gave me heaven instead.**

**Is the breastplate of righteousness on my chest?
Uh-huh! You can see that I'm wearin' God's best.**

**Is the belt of truth tied around my waist?
Uh-huh! I'm wrapped up in God's grace.**

**Is the shield of faith strapped on my arm?
Uh-huh! Satan's arrows will do me no harm.**

**Is the gospel of peace what I'm wearin' for shoes?
Uh-huh! And I'm prepared to tell the good news.**

**Thank you, God, for these good gifts!
Help me live as you want me to live.**

CLOSING

Gotcha Covered

Say: **Be sure to use your Good News Shoes this week, because ★ God wants us to spread the good news.**

Have the kids take the scrolls from their Good News Shoes, and form groups of eight or fewer. Let each child pick one of the items of good news from the scrolls to thank God for. Have each group pray together.

Then gather kids in a large circle, and close with a prayer similar to this one: **Dear Lord, thank you for making us your messengers. Help us use our Good News Shoes to talk to people who need to hear about you. And please protect us with all the other pieces of armor, too. In Jesus' name, amen.**

GOOD NEWS SHOES

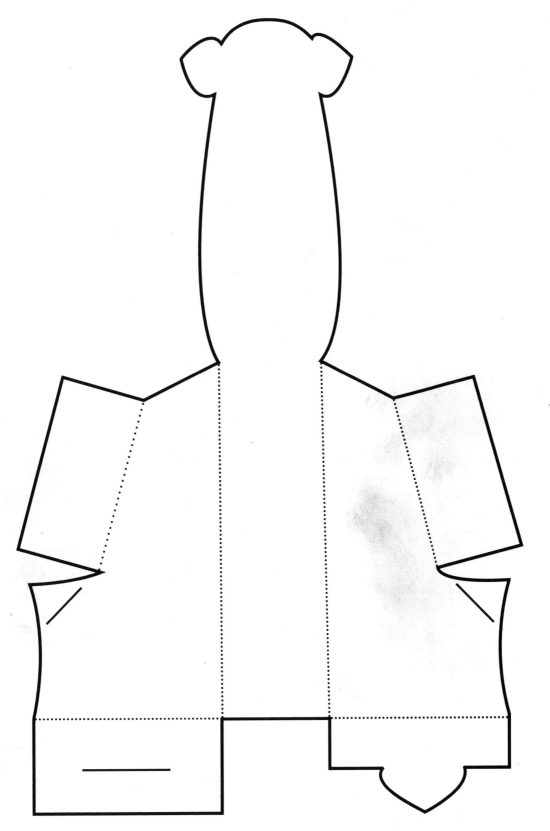

GOOD NEWS SCROLLS

"The Savior—yes, the Messiah, the Lord—has been born today in Bethlehem, the city of David! And you will recognize him by this sign: You will find a baby wrapped snugly in strips of cloth, lying in a manger" (Luke 2:11-12).

"Coming to his hometown, he began teaching the people in their synagogue, and they were amazed. `Where did this man get this wisdom and these miraculous powers?' they asked. 'Isn't this the carpenter's son?'" (Matthew 13:54-55, NIV).

"A vast crowd brought to him people who were lame, blind, crippled, those who couldn't speak, and many others. They laid them before Jesus, and he healed them all" (Matthew 15:30).

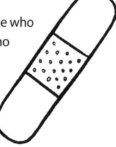

"I am the good shepherd. The good shepherd sacrifices his life for the sheep" (John 10:11).

"Jesus replied, 'All who love me will do what I say. My Father will love him, and we will come and make our home with each of them'" (John 14:23).

"There is no greater love than to lay down one's life for one's friends" (John 15:13).

"But God showed his great love for us by sending Christ to die for us while we were still sinners" (Romans 5:8).

"If you confess with your mouth that Jesus is Lord and believe in your heart that God raised him from the dead, you will be saved" (Romans 10:9).

"He humbled himself in obedience to God and died a criminal's death on a cross! Therefore, God elevated him to the place of highest honor

and gave him the name above all other names, that at the name of Jesus every knee should bow, in heaven and on earth and under the earth, and every tongue confess that Jesus Christ is Lord, to the glory of God the Father" (Philippians 2:8-11).

LESSON AIM

To help kids understand that ★God's Word makes us strong.

OBJECTIVES

Kids will

- ✓ blow paper cups over and then see that cups are stronger when they are filled with liquid,
- ✓ discover how God's Word helped Peter and John,
- ✓ learn how God's Word can make them strong today, and
- ✓ commit to wearing the armor of God.

YOU'LL NEED

- ❑ medium-size paper cups
- ❑ a watch with a second hand
- ❑ a sports drink such as Powerade or Gatorade*
- ❑ Bibles
- ❑ photocopies of the "Sword of the Spirit" handout (p. 48)
- ❑ scissors

*Always check for allergies before serving snacks.

BIBLE BASIS

Acts 3:1–4:22

When Peter and John healed a well-known crippled beggar who proceeded to walk and leap around the Temple courts expressing his praise, the crowds at the Temple stood agape with wonder. Like a good preacher, Peter lost no time in proclaiming that this amazing feat had been done in the name of Jesus Christ. It was no surprise when the Temple guards escorted Peter and John to a nice, quiet cell for the remainder of the day. Early the next morning, the Sanhedrin assembled to question these "culprits" about their act of kindness to a lame man.

all-in-one
SUNDAY
SCHOOL

Did Peter and John have reason to be nervous? You bet! This was the very court that had demanded the death sentence for Jesus—and not so very long before. By all human expectations, this dynamic duo should have been drenched in perspiration. But when Peter quoted Scripture in the power of the Holy Spirit, supported by the prayers of the church, it was the members of the Sanhedrin who started to sweat! Peter and John spoke with such authority that the highest court in the land marveled at these "unschooled" men, and noted that they had been with Jesus. God's Word indeed makes us strong!

Ephesians 6:17-18

Paul finalizes his description of God's armor by admonishing us to take the sword of the Spirit. Other Scriptures pair God's Word with forceful imagery as well. Jeremiah 23:29 asks: " 'Does not my word burn like fire?' says the Lord. 'Is it not like a mighty hammer that smashes a rock to pieces?' " Hebrews 4:12 states: "For the word of God is alive and powerful. It is sharper than the sharpest two-edged sword, cutting between soul and spirit, between joint and marrow. It exposes our innermost thoughts and desires." God's Word is no benign book filled with suggestions on how to live. God's truth packs a punch that can't be ducked, sidestepped, or otherwise avoided. There's no doubting its power. It's a piece of God's armor that every Christian needs to have well in hand.

UNDERSTANDING YOUR KIDS

Many times in their lives, your kids have felt powerless. Violence and greed seem to rule the world, even in elementary school. Families separate, and children are left to contemplate what they could have done to prevent it. Nuclear and biological weapons dominate news reports and nightmares. But none of those great evils can stand before the awesome power of God's eternal, unchanging, life-giving Word. Your kids need to know that real power comes from the sword of the Spirit—and you're going to tell them this week.

 **The Lesson**

ATTENTION GRABBER

Blow Me Down!

Before class, set at least a dozen paper cups in a row along the edge of a table. As kids arrive, challenge them to estimate how many cups they can blow over or blow across the table in 15 seconds. Let children take turns kneeling in front of the table and blowing over as many cups as they can. If time permits, let those who want to improve their scores try again.

Ask:

♦ **If we try this again, do you think you can blow over as many cups as you did before?**

Let each child name the number of cups he or she will blow over in the next round. Replace the cups on the edge of the table; then bring out bottles of sports drink, and fill each cup at least half full. Say: **Okay, we're all set. Who wants to go first?**

Let volunteers try to blow the cups over. Of course, the liquid will weight the cups down and keep them solidly in place. After kids have tried in vain to blow the cups over, say: **After all that blowing, you're probably thirsty. Help yourself to a cup of sports drink.** Then ask:

♦ **How did the sports drink affect the cups?** (It made them heavier; it kept them from getting blown over.)

♦ **What is sports drink supposed to do for people who drink it?** (Make them stronger; give them energy.)

♦ **Do you believe sports drink can do all those things for you?** (Yeah, it makes me feel better; no, it doesn't really do that much.)

Say: **Sports drinks claim to make us strong. I don't know if they can really do that or not. But today we're going to learn about something that does make us strong. And it keeps us from getting blown over by difficult things that happen in life. It's the last piece of the armor of God. Actually, there are several of them in this room.**

♦ **Can anyone guess what I'm talking about?**

Let kids guess. If no one points out a Bible, pick up one yourself and say: **The last piece of armor is the sword of the Spirit, the Word of God. Let's get going with our Bible story and discover how ★ God's Word makes us strong.**

Teacher Tip

Place the cups on the forward edge of the table so that when kids blow them over, they'll remain on the table top. Have volunteer spotters stand around the table to catch any cups that roll toward the edge.

BIBLE STUDY

Trouble at the Temple (Acts 3:1–4:22)

Before class photocopy the "Trouble at the Temple" story. Cut apart the 15 verses. Have kids form trios. If the number of kids in your class isn't divisible by three, form one group of two or four. Place nonreaders with readers. Distribute the verses of the story as evenly as possible among the trios.

Say: **Decide which member of your trio will be the reader. The other two members will lead the motions. I'll give you a couple of minutes to go over your verses together.**

Have all the trios stand in one circle in the order of their verses. Explain that everyone will do the motions with the trio that's performing.

When the trios are ready, introduce the story by saying: **Our story is about two Bible heroes who got into big trouble for doing good. But this dynamic duo never wavered or ran away, because they knew ★God's Word makes us strong.**

You may want to let kids perform the story twice so they get a good grasp of the plot. At the end of the story, lead everyone in a round of applause. Then have trios scatter around the room. Ask these questions, pausing after each one to allow time for discussion.

♦ **How did Peter and John make the priests angry?** (They healed a man and then said they did it by faith in Jesus; they said Jesus came back to life.)

♦ **Why were Peter and John thrown in jail?** (To stop them from telling people about Jesus; to shut them up.)

♦ **Why was it so scary for them to be brought before the court?** (This was the same court that had put Jesus to death; members of the court were dangerous enemies of Jesus.)

♦ **How did Peter and John surprise the members of the court?** (They weren't scared; they were smart and strong.)

♦ **Why weren't Peter and John scared?** (Because they had faith in Jesus; God's Word helped them know what to say.)

♦ **How could you be as brave as Peter and John?** (Kids' answers will vary.)

Say: **Peter and John stood strong in the face of pretty scary circumstances. Their strength came from knowing that they were right because they had God's Word to back them up and because they had been with Jesus.**

LIFE APPLICATION

Give Me Strength

Say: **The high court Peter and John appeared before was called the Sanhedrin. The members of the Sanhedrin tried**

TROUBLE AT THE TEMPLE

1 Peter and John went to the Temple for prayer.
(Fold hands.)
A poor man who couldn't walk sat begging there.
(Point to one side.)
Whenever people passed him by, the beggar would say,
(Walk two fingers across your palm.)
"Alms for the poor! A few coins today?"
(Cup hands as if begging.)

2 Neither Peter nor John had money to spare,
(Hold out empty hands.)
But they had something else they were happy to share.
(Cross arms and nod head.)
Peter said, "In Jesus' name, get up and walk."
(Pretend to pull someone up.)
When the man jumped up, how people did gawk!
(Look surprised and point.)

3 The healed man jumped and leaped and praised.
(Jump and wave arms.)
The people who saw it were truly amazed!
(Look wide-eyed; cover cheeks with hands.)
"How did he do that?" everyone wondered.
(Scratch head.)
"By faith in Jesus," Peter's voice thundered.
(Point upward.)

4 Peter and John were in big trouble now.
(Shake finger.)
The priests hated Jesus, uh-huh, and how!
(Cross arms and look mean.)
"Seize them," cried a priest. "Go quickly and arrest them!
(Sweep arm to the right and point.)
Throw the culprits into jail! How we detest them!"
(Shake fists.)

5 So Peter and John spent that night in a cell,
(Pretend to hang on to bars.)
But the very next day they had a story to tell.
(Nod head.)
For early in the morning they got this command:
(Rub eyes.)
You must stand before the highest court in the land.
(Sweep arm to the left and point.)

6 That was the court that had put Jesus to death!
(Cover mouth in surprise.)
But Peter just smiled and took a deep breath.
(Smile; take a deep breath.)
A friend stood nearby on two legs that were strong—
(Stomp one foot and then the other.)
The healed man had come to right this wrong.
(Point to legs; nod.)

(continued)

7 God's Spirit filled Peter; then he began to speak.
(Raise hands, and then cover heart.)
Peter felt courageous—not frightened or weak.
(Flex arm muscles.)
"This man stands before you—he used to be lame.
(Gesture to the right.)
How was he healed? By the power of Jesus' name!"
(Raise fist toward heaven.)

8 The priests all mumbled and grumbled and shuffled.
(Shake head and mumble.)
They didn't like Jesus! Their feathers were ruffled!
(Cross arms and look mean.)
Then Peter spoke again, straight from God's Word—
(Pretend to hold open Bible.)
A passage from Psalms he knew the priests had heard.
(Point to pretend Bible.)

9 "You rejected Jesus—now he's at the head.
(Point straight ahead and then up.)
You hung him on a cross, but God raised him from the dead!"
(Make cross with arms; raise hands toward heaven.)
Peter wasn't scared, though the court members raved.
(Wave arms angrily.)
He continued, "It's in Jesus' name that you must be saved!"
(Make cross with arms.)

10 The judges surely knew that their actions were wrong.
(Scratch head and look unhappy.)
Speaking from God's Word had made Peter strong.
(Pretend to hold open Bible; flex arm muscles.)
So the high priest said, "That's all we'll hear today."
(Cover ears.)
Then he called the Temple guards to take the men away.
(Walk fingers across palm.)

11 One priest said, "These men have never been to school.
(Tap head.)
How is it they can challenge us? We're the ones who rule!"
(Point thumb to chest.)
Then another said, "This is why they're so brave:
(Shake finger.)
They've been with Jesus; they said he rose from the grave."
(Make cross with arms; raise hands toward heaven.)

12 A Sadducee spoke up and asked, "What shall we do?
(Shrug shoulders.)
The whole city knows of their miracle—it's true!"
(Spread arms wide.)
"I know what to do," said another. "Let's scare them;
(Make mean face and claws.)
Say that if they preach again, we'll punish them—not spare them."
(Pretend to slap someone.)

13 When Peter and John were called back into the room,
(Walk fingers across palm.)
A loud, angry voice began to shout at them and boom.
(Cup hands around mouth.)
The angry judge warned them, "If you two want to please us,
(Shake finger.)
You'll never, never preach again in the name of Jesus."
(Shake head.)

14 Peter calmly said, "You must judge what is right:
(Point straight ahead with two fingers.)
To obey God or obey you—what's best in God's sight?
(Point toward heaven with two fingers.)
Don't even try to tell us not to say another word,
(Cover mouth and shake head.)
For we cannot stop speaking of the things we've seen and heard."
(Pull hand away; spread arms wide.)

15 There was no stopping Peter; there was no stopping John.
(Point to one side and then the other.)
God's Word made them strong—they'd preach on and on!
(Flex arm muscles.)

to make life hard for the early Christians. They wanted to stop the gospel of Christ from spreading any further than it already had. What happened to Peter and John happened to lots of other Christians as well. They were arrested, threatened, thrown in jail, beaten, sometimes even killed. Jesus' enemies were sure that this kind of treatment would stomp out Christianity before it even got started. Ask:

♦ **What gave them the strength to keep going in the face of prison and death threats?** (God's power; the Holy Spirit helped them.)

Say: **These early Christians had God's armor on. They carried the sword of the Spirit, which is the Word of God. And nothing could defeat them—not threats, not beatings, not prison, not even death!**

♦ **Where are places that Christians face those kinds of threats today?** (China; Muslim countries.)

♦ **When is it hard to stand strong for the Lord in our town? at your school? in your neighborhood?** (When bullies threaten me; when people use bad language; when people make fun of me because I'm a Christian; when teachers say the Bible isn't true.)

Say: **Let's form a circle. Now, without touching anyone, stretch your arms straight out at shoulder level, palms up,** and hold that position. Good. Now while we're holding our arms like this, we'll take turns naming things that make it hard for us to stand strong for God today. It's fine to mention some of the things we just talked about. I'll begin; then we'll go around the circle to my right.

Encourage kids to mention things such as getting teased about their faith, hearing people use God's name when they swear, being asked to cheat, being in a group that picks on people, and being invited to watch R-rated movies. After everyone has mentioned something, ask:

♦ **How are your arms feeling?** (Tired; sore.)

Say: ★ **God's Word makes us strong. To feel what that's like, rest your arms on the shoulders of the people on either side of you. Doesn't that feel great? God's Word gives us that kind of help and support when we're feeling weak and discouraged. Let's find out exactly how God's Word can help us.**

COMMITMENT

Grab That Sword!

Distribute scissors and the "Sword of the Spirit" handout.

Say: **Fold your handouts in half the long way, right down the center of the open Bible.** Pause for children to do that. **Now cut the Bible at the top from the center to the corner. Then cut at the bottom from the center to the corner.**

When kids have completed these cuts, have them open their handouts and fold up on both edges of the open Bible. Then have them fold down on the inside edges of the Bible. Demonstrate how to fold the handout into a card by folding it in half on the dotted line and then folding it closed with the Bible on the inside. When the card is opened, the Bible will pop up.

Direct kids' attention to the verse printed on the open Bible. Have a volunteer read the verse aloud. Then ask:

♦ **Put that verse in your own words.** (God's Word is alive and very powerful; it helps us know what's right and wrong.)

Say: **We'll find more information about God's Word on the back of this card.** Have volunteers read the verses aloud. Then challenge kids to explain the verses in their own words. Ask:

♦ **What do we need to do for God's Word to be powerful and active in our lives?** (We need to read it; we need to remember what it says; we need to live the way the Bible tells us to.)

Say: **Great! And when we do those things, we allow God's Word to work in our lives, and then ★ God's Word makes us strong.**

CLOSING

Rapping Up

Say: **Now we've talked about the whole armor of God. When you wear this armor, you're ready to face anything! We have one more verse to learn in our "Armor of God Rap." Here it is. Repeat after me.**

> Got the sword of the Spirit, God's Holy Word?
> Uh-huh! And it's full of God's power, I've heard.

Say: **Good job! Now let's do our "Armor of God Rap" one last time.**

Review the rap verses that kids have learned previously; then have fun marching in creative ways around the class as you lead the rap in a cadence rhythm:

> I don't know, but I've been told
> The armor of God makes me strong and *bold!*

> See the helmet of salvation on my head?
> God took my sins and gave me heaven instead.

> Is the breastplate of righteousness on my chest?
> Uh-huh! You can see that I'm wearin' God's best.

> Is the belt of truth tied around my waist?
> Uh-huh! I'm wrapped up in God's grace.

> Is the shield of faith strapped on my arm?
> Uh-huh! Satan's arrows will do me no harm.

> Is the gospel of peace what I'm wearin' for shoes?
> Uh-huh! And I'm prepared to tell the good news.

> Got the sword of the Spirit, God's Holy Word?
> Uh-huh! And it's full of God's power, I've heard.

> Thank you, God, for these good gifts
> Help me live as you want me to live.

Say: **That was awesome! I hope you'll remember this rap, because it will remind you to take the armor of God with you wherever you go. The words are printed on the front of the cards you just made.**

And keep on studying God's Word because ★ God's Word…(pause and let kids finish along with you) **makes us strong!**

Remind kids to take their "Sword of the Spirit" handouts as they go.

THE ARMOR OF GOD RAP

*I don't know, but I've been told
The armor of God makes me strong and bold!*

*See the helmet of salvation on my head?
God took my sins and gave me heaven instead.*

*Is the breastplate of righteousness on my chest?
Uh-huh! You can see that I'm wearin' God's best.*

*Is the belt of truth tied around my waist?
Uh-huh! I'm wrapped up in God's grace.*

*Is the shield of faith strapped on my arm?
Uh-huh! Satan's arrows will do me no harm.*

*Is the gospel of peace what I'm wearin' for shoes?
Uh-huh! And I'm prepared to tell the good news.*

*Got the sword of the Spirit, God's Holy Word?
Uh-huh! And it's full of God's power, I've heard.*

*Thank you, God, for these good gifts!
Help me live as you want me to live.*

"Every word of God proves true. He defends all who come to him for protection" (Proverbs 30:5, The Living Bible).

"When you received the word of God, which you heard from us, you accepted it not as the word of men, but as it actually is, the word of God, which is at work in you who believe" (1 Thessalonians 2:13, NIV).

"For you have been born again, but not to a life that will quickly end. Your new life will last forever because it comes from the eternal, living word of God. As Scriptures say, 'People are like grass, their glory is like a flower in the field. The grass withers and the flower fades. But the word of the Lord remains forever.'" (1 Peter 1:23-25).

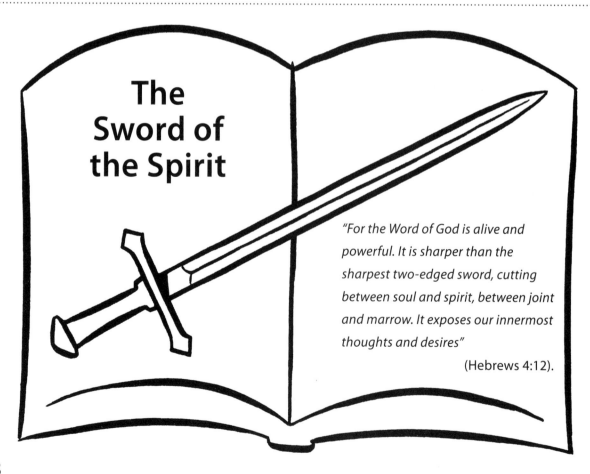

The
Sword of
the Spirit

"For the Word of God is alive and powerful. It is sharper than the sharpest two-edged sword, cutting between soul and spirit, between joint and marrow. It exposes our innermost thoughts and desires" (Hebrews 4:12).

LESSON AIM

To help kids learn that ★ it's good to celebrate the ways God blesses us.

OBJECTIVES

Kids or families will

✓ experience not being thanked for their efforts and then being thanked,

✓ examine and re-create the Feast of Tabernacles,

✓ create personal expressions of thanks to God, and

✓ commit to a thankful lifestyle.

Teacher Tip

This lesson works well with an intergenerational class. You may wish to invite whole families to join you for this session.

YOU'LL NEED

❏ bedsheets, blankets, or small tents

❏ Bibles

❏ newsprint

❏ a marker

❏ a toy horn

❏ grapes, olives, dates, and soda crackers*

❏ juice*

❏ paper cups and plates

❏ photocopies of the "Celebration Bag" handout (p. 56)

❏ pencils

❏ scissors

❏ old newspapers or scrap paper

❏ glue sticks

❏ shiny red, white, and blue gift bag stuffing

*Always check for allergies before serving snacks.

all-in-one
SUNDAY
SCHOOL

Deuteronomy 16:13-17; Nehemiah 8:13-18

The Feast of Tabernacles (also called the Festival of Shelters) is a fascinating Jewish festival. Unlike our Thanksgiving celebration, the Feast of Tabernacles lasted seven days, from the 15th to the 21st day of Tishri, our October. During this feast the Israelites traveled to Jerusalem where they celebrated the harvest of fruits and olives. They built and camped out in outdoor shelters called "booths" to commemorate the 40 years their ancestors had lived in temporary shelters as they wandered in the wilderness. Shelters were located on rooftops, in courtyards, in the court of the temple, and along the edges of city streets. In the evenings the people lit torches and danced and sang in the streets. On the eighth day, they took the shelters down and gathered at the temple to worship.

It's wonderful to celebrate God's goodness with feasting, fireworks and parades. If you're teaching these lessons openly, you live in a culture blessed with the freedom to honor God and share his Word. What a blessing! Pop a firecracker! I'm a citizen of the USA, so I think of this lesson in terms of a fourth of July celebration. But, knowing these books travel around the world, I heartily encourage you to adapt the content to suit a national celebration in your own country.

To the Israelites, national and religious celebrations were one and the same. With God as their leader, the entire nation survived 40 years in the wilderness. Then came the unprecendented conquest and occupation of Canaan. The Israelites didn't have Moses Day or Joshua Day. Instead they celebrated the God who guided them, provided for them and kept them together as a people during this generation-long desert sojourn.

During national celebrations we can acknowledge the times God intervened on behalf of our people and thank him for wise leaders and for the abundance and freedom we enjoy. How long do you think we would have survived a 40-year desert sojourn? Yikes! I always give myself a big pat on the back for a few days of tent camping in our cool, well-watered Colorado mountains!

During our first post-seminary years, my husband and I served as missionaries in the far east. Tall, fair-skinned Christians were certainly the oddity in our community, but we very seldom faced any hostility. At one point, however, a flight itinerary took us to a nearby country where tight military control was the order of the day. I will never forget having a machine gun trained on me as I descended the steps from the airplane, or having a soldier knock my camera away when my telephoto lens was evidently pointed in a forbidden direction. That day gave me an indelible sense of thankfulness for what we in North America take for granted with rarely a second thought. This Biblical feast challenges you: Give it a thought! We enjoy extraordinary blessings that much of the world only dreams of!

As we celebrate important national holidays, let's not forget to thank God for his role in our history and the ongoing abundance he provides.

Psalm 67

The psalms are rich with praise and are meaningful for people of all generations and all nations. This psalm celebrates God's goodness with joy and thanksgiving for a good harvest and God's blessing on his world.

UNDERSTANDING YOUR KIDS

Ah, there's nothing like the glorious freedom of summer capped by a holiday that celebrates the glorious freedom of our nation! The fruits of the harvest are many: watermelon, blueberries and strawberries, early sweet corn—yum! Most of the kids who run and shriek with the many delights of our national holiday lack any clue of how privileged they are compared to vast numbers of children in the world. Why has God chosen to so bless us? I have no answer, just thanks.

Use this lesson to teach kids that the Fourth of July is not only a time to celebrate, but a time to worship and give thanks to our God who has chosen to abundantly bless us.

The Lesson 😊

ATTENTION GRABBER

Thanks/No Thanks

During this lesson, participants will put together "booths" to re-create the biblical Feast of Tabernacles. The booths can be made by simply draping sheets or blankets over tables and chairs, by putting up lightweight tents, or even by hanging small tents from the ceiling. Make the process as simple or as sophisticated as you like.

You'll need one booth for every four to six people. Decide where you'll have the booths set up—in the corners of the room, for instance. Leave the room in its usual configuration for the Attention Grabber.

When participants arrive, have everyone who has shoes that tie stand against one wall. Have everyone with slip-on shoes stand against the opposite wall. It's okay if the groups are unequal in size.

Turn to the group with shoes that tie and say: **Ties, I'd like you to help me rearrange the tables and chairs. Please move them to the other end of the room.**

After they perform this task, shrug your shoulders and shake your head.

Then turn to the other group and say: **Okay, No-Ties, I've changed my mind. I really liked the tables and chairs the way they were. Would you put them back, please?** When the No-Ties finish their task, thank them enthusiastically. Pat them on their backs and shake hands with several of them.

Turn back to the Ties and say: **Okay, now I've got it figured out. I need one table in each corner** (or however you want to arrange the room for creating the booths) **and the chairs here in a semicircle.**

When the Ties complete this task, say: **That's a great job! Thanks for sticking with me! I really appreciate your helpful attitude.**

Have everyone sit down. Then ask:

♦ **Ties, how did it feel when you did what I asked without being thanked for it?** (Kind of disappointing; a little confusing.)

♦ **How did you feel when I did say thank you?** (I was glad that I helped you; I felt appreciated.)

♦ **How do you react when you do something nice for someone but that person doesn't thank you?** (It's okay, because it was my choice to help; I might not feel so friendly toward that person again.)

♦ **Tell me about a time when you got a note or other**

special thank-you from someone. Kids' answers will vary.

Say: ★ It's good to give thanks. We like it when people thank us for what we do, and we sometimes feel bad if people don't notice or don't care. God likes it when we thank him, too. Today we're going to learn about a special feast the Israelites celebrated to give thanks to God.

BIBLE STUDY

Welcome to the Feast! (Deuteronomy 16:13-17; Nehemiah 8:13-18; Psalm 67)

Say: Let's find out about this feast straight from the Bible. Listen carefully to what the Bible says, because I'm going to ask you what it tells us to do for our feast.

Have volunteers read aloud Deuteronomy 16:13-17 and Nehemiah 8:13-18. Explain that Festival of Shelters is another name for Feast of Tabernacles. Then ask:

♦ What do we need to do to celebrate the Feast of Tabernacles? (Get branches to build booths; read from the Bible; celebrate joyfully; thank God for the harvest; bring gifts.)

List participants' answers on a sheet of newsprint.

Say: Before you leave class today, we'll do all these things. Let's begin by asking God to bless our feast time.

Ask a volunteer to pray or pray a simple prayer yourself, asking God to bless your time of giving thanks.

After the prayer, bring out your toy horn and blow it. Explain that Jewish priests used to blow a ram's horn to call people to worship, and that whenever you blow your horn, everyone should stop what they're doing and focus on you.

Then say: Now we need to build our booths.

Help participants form groups of four to six people. Ask each group to choose a feast maker, a reader, and two or more booth builders. Show the readers and the booth builders the materials you've provided for making booths—tents to assemble or bedsheets and blankets to drape over tables and chairs.

As the readers and booth builders work on the booths, set out grapes, olives, dates, soda crackers, juice, paper cups, and paper plates. Have the feast makers prepare a plate of food and cups of juice for the people in their groups.

When the booths are complete and the feast prepared, blow the toy horn to bring everyone together. Say: It's time for the feast! The food we have here is like foods people enjoyed in Bible times. Help your feast maker carry the feast into your booth. Readers, before anyone eats, please read Psalm 67 aloud. Listen carefully as your reader reads Psalm 67 and bow your heads in worship. Then say "amen" together. After that, you're welcome to sample your Bible-times feast. ★ It's good to celebrate the ways God blesses us!

Teacher Tip

Encourage adults that have joined you to mix things up and get in groups with kids from other families and to act as helpers and facilitators. Try to have a variety of ages within groups. Women in dresses might prefer to be "feast makers" rather than sit on the floor in booths.

LIFE APPLICATION

Celebration Psalms

Allow up to five minutes for groups to read Scripture and enjoy the Bible-times foods. Then blow the horn.

Say: **Stay in your booths. In just a moment, I'm going to ask you to send one of your booth builders to come pick up pencils, scissors, and "Celebration Bag" handouts. You'll find directions for writing your own psalm of thanks on the handout. The readers and writers in your group can help those who don't yet read and write. When you're finished, cut and glue your celebration bags together, and then read each other the psalms you've written.**

Have each group send a booth builder to pick up supplies. As participants work, circulate among the booths to offer encouragement and suggestions.

As you see groups finishing, blow the horn and announce that there are two minutes left. Then blow the horn again to bring everyone together. Invite volunteers to read their psalms to the whole group.

After volunteers have shared, say: ★ **It's good to celebrate the way God blesses us! Now let's stuff those bags with some Fourth of July fun!**

Let kids fill their bags with shiny red, white and blue gift bag stuffing.

COMMITMENT

Paper Offerings

Refer to the list you created that describes the Feast of Tabernacles. Point out that you've done most of the things on the list. Ask:

♦ **What do we need to do to complete our celebration?** (Give gifts to God.)

Set out piles of old newspapers or scrap paper. Have participants crumple, cut, or tear the paper to create sculptures of things they're thankful for. You might demonstrate by making a crumpled paper sculpture in front of the class.

Allow two or three minutes for participants to work. Then say: **Let's line up and present our sculptures to God as gifts of thanks.**

Lead the procession by walking to the front of the room, placing your sculpture on the table, and saying: **God, I thank you for** [whatever your sculpture represents]**.** Then walk to the back of the room and signal the next participant to go forward. Encourage an atmosphere of quiet worship.

Teacher Tip

If it's in keeping with your church's tradition and your participants would enjoy it, you might invite someone to lead the class in a simple dance to Jewish music. Have participants wrap their arms around each other's shoulders, then use the "step, cross behind, step, cross in front, step, cross behind, step, kick, then reverse" pattern to create a joyful expression of praise.

CLOSING

Everyday Celebrations

After all the sculptures have been presented, gather everyone around them.

Say: ★ **It's good to celebrate the ways God blesses us. And we don't have to wait for a national holiday or a feast day to do it!**

Allow a minute for partners to share; then invite volunteers to share their ideas with the class.

Close with a prayer similar to this one: **Lord, you truly are a great God. Thank you for all the ways you show that you love us. Thank you for the good food we have to eat and the wonderful country we live in. Help us to remember to thank you every day. In Jesus' name, amen.**

Tell participants you'd be very thankful for help in taking down the booths. Encourage everyone to take their sculptures with them as reminders of God's goodness.

CELEBRATION BAG

Cut out the bag on the solid lines. Then write your own psalm by finishing the phrases on the sides. Fold in on the dotted lines, and pull the squares to the inside and glue them.

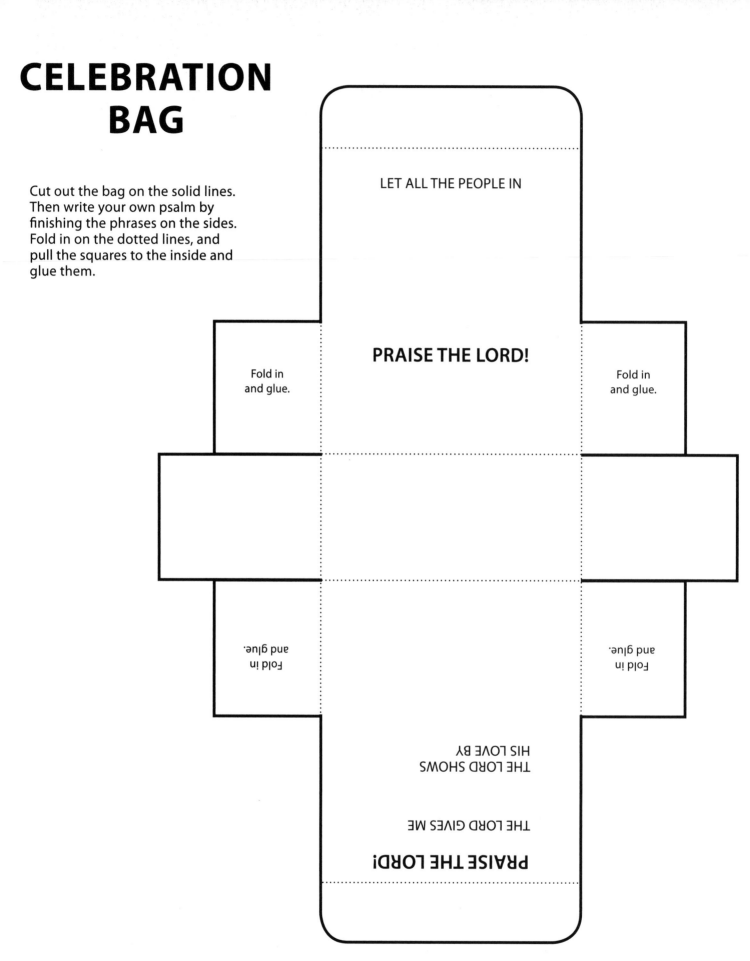

LET ALL THE PEOPLE IN

PRAISE THE LORD!

Fold in and glue.

Fold in and glue.

Fold in and glue.

Fold in and glue.

THE LORD SHOWS
HIS LOVE BY

THE LORD GIVES ME

PRAISE THE LORD!

LESSON AIM

To help kids understand that ★ it's important to listen to God.

OBJECTIVES

Kids will

✓ come to see the Bible as God's personal word to them,
✓ present commercials about the benefits of God's Word,
✓ practice listening prayers, and
✓ plan a personal quiet time.

YOU'LL NEED

❑ a honeycomb or jar of honey*
❑ graham crackers*
❑ Bibles
❑ plastic knives
❑ paper plates
❑ damp washcloths
❑ a large white onion
❑ hexagons cut from yellow construction paper
❑ pencils
❑ tape
❑ photocopies of the "I'm Listening, Lord" mini-journal (p. 64)
*Always check for allergies before serving snacks.

BIBLE BASIS

Psalm 119:97-104

Psalm 119 is unique in several ways. It's the longest chapter in Scripture, and it's also an acrostic. Each stanza starts with one of the 22 letters of the Hebrew alphabet. But most significant is this psalm's unique theme of praise to God for his Word. Unlike other psalms that focus on what God has done and is doing, Psalm 119 gives praise to God's Word and the help and guidance it brings to our lives.

all-in-one
SUNDAY
SCHOOL

1 Samuel 3:2-11

The remarkable thing about this familiar story is God bypassed a priest and gave a message of great importance to a child. It's never too early for children to learn to listen for God's voice—and to obey it.

UNDERSTANDING YOUR KIDS

Kids are constantly bombarded with auditory and visual stimuli. Just watch 15 minutes of Saturday-morning television sometime, and see if you can keep pace with everything that's happening! Or watch five minutes of one of their video games without having your eyes crossed!

The challenge for us as Christian teachers is to get kids to see that spending a few quiet moments with God each day can make a tremendous difference in their lives. With no commercials, jingles, or two-for-one offers to entice them, kids need to see there's eternal hope, help, and unending love just waiting to be tapped.

Younger kids will benefit from your making available a variety of Bible-story books for them to borrow. Then they can follow through on the principles they'll learn in this session.

Older kids need concrete guidance about how and when to approach daily Bible study and prayer. Many Christian educators direct upper-elementary kids to the books of Psalms and James for their first ventures into independent Bible study. The "I'm Listening, Lord" mini-journal will be an excellent tool to help your kids get started with a daily quiet time.

 **The Lesson**

ATTENTION GRABBER

Listen Up

Ask for a volunteer to leave the room. Choose an older child who will reliably follow your directions. When the volunteer has left, show the rest of the kids where you're going to hide the honey and graham crackers.

Say: **When [name] comes back, you're going to try to guide [him or her] to the honey and graham crackers by giving the clues "hot" and "cold." No fair moving or pointing or giving any other clues. If [name] finds the honey and graham crackers within 30 seconds, everyone gets to share them.**

Slip into the hall with the volunteer. Quickly explain he or she is just to stroll around the classroom and completely ignore the clues the other kids are giving.

Bring the volunteer back into the classroom.

Say: **Is everybody ready? The 30 seconds starts ... now!**

Notify kids when you're down to 20 and 15 seconds. Then as their excitement mounts, count down the seconds from 10 to zero. Have everyone, including your volunteer, sit down. Warn kids that the location of the honey and graham crackers must still be kept secret. Ask:

♦ **What was it like as [name] ignored your clues?** (Frustrating, I felt like I had to yell louder.)

♦ **What's so bad about [name] not paying attention to what you were saying?** (Now we don't get the snack.)

♦ **How is [name] ignoring your directions like people who live their lives without paying any attention to what God has to say to them?** (They miss out on good things, too.)

Say: **Okay, let's play this game again. This time, [name], pay attention to the clues the kids are giving you.**

Let the kids call out "hot" and "cold" again to lead the volunteer to the honey and graham crackers. Have everyone give the volunteer a big round of applause. Then gather kids in a circle, place the honey and graham crackers in the center and ask:

♦ **How did you feel as [name] got closer and closer to the honey and graham crackers?** (Happy; excited.)

♦ **How is that like being tuned in to what God has to say to you?** (It's exciting; neat things happen to us.)

♦ **What are some ways we can tune in to God?** (Reading the Bible; praying.)

Say: **We're going to eat the honey and graham crackers in just a minute, but first, let's look at something the Bible says.**

> **Teacher Tip**
>
> *If kids in your class are younger or especially excitable, you might have them sit on their hands before bringing the volunteer back into the room.*

BIBLE STUDY

Tuning In to God
(1 Samuel 3:2-11; Psalm 119:97-104)

Have kids turn their Bibles to Psalm 119:97-104. Have older kids read the psalm aloud, each reading one verse.

After the reading, bring out plastic knives and paper plates. If you were able to obtain a honeycomb, let kids examine it. Some kids may be able to explain how and why the bees construct the honeycomb.

Have kids each dip a knife into the honey and spread the honey onto a graham cracker.

As kids are enjoying their snacks, say: **Oh no! I forgot! Would anyone rather have this for a treat?** Pull out a big white onion. Kids will probably laugh as they assure you they'd rather have the honey and graham crackers. Ask:

♦ **What's so good about honey?** (It's sweet; it's good for you.)

♦ **How is learning what the Bible says like eating honey?** (It's good and good for us; we don't want to stop.)

♦ **Why did the psalm writer compare reading the Bible to eating honey?** (Honey is a delicious treat; it's sweet and rich and good, like God's Word.)

♦ **What good things do you get from honey?** (Energy; vitamins.)

♦ **What good things do you get from reading the Bible?** (I learn about God's love; I get guidance for my life; I get comfort when I'm feeling sad.)

Pass out pencils. Ask kids to write (or draw symbols of) their responses on yellow construction paper hexagons and tape them to the wall. Explain that hexagons represent the honey and the honeycomb the psalm writer was talking about.

Say: **That's pretty sweet stuff! Let's look back at this psalm for a minute.** Ask:

♦ **What does the psalm writer say reading God's Word does for him?** (It makes him wiser than his enemies; it gives him understanding; it keeps him from doing evil.)

Have kids write or draw these responses on yellow hexagons and add them to the honeycomb wall.

Say: **God talks to us through his Word. The Bible is like a personal letter written to each one of us. You know how fun it is to get letters in the mail—imagine getting a letter from God! You'd want to read it every day, over and over again. And I hope you will. ★ It's important to listen to God.**

God talks to us in other ways, too—especially through prayer.

Hexagon

60

Ask:

♦ **What do you pray about when you pray?** (I thank God for the things he gives me; I ask him for things I need; I ask him to take care of my friends and family.)

Say: **Did you ever think of listening to God in prayer? Let's learn about someone in the Bible who listened to God— someone who may have been close to your age.**

Have older kids open their Bibles to 1 Samuel 3:2-11. Choose kids to read the parts of the narrator, Samuel, God, and Eli. Be ready to signal the characters as their turns come to read. Position four chairs as corners of a big square. Dim the lights, if possible, to fit the setting of the story. Have the readers sit on the chairs, with the other kids on the floor in the middle.

When everyone is in place, introduce the story this way:

Samuel was a boy whose mother sent him to serve the Lord when he was still very young. He was raised by an old priest named Eli. So Samuel grew up in the temple. This story happened late one night. Shh! It's very dark in the temple ... and very quiet ... and young Samuel is just about to fall asleep.

Signal the readers to begin.

After the reading, explain that God went on to tell Samuel how the family of Eli would be punished for breaking God's laws. Then ask:

♦ **Why was Samuel confused about who was calling him?** (He'd never heard God talking to him before.)

♦ **Why is nighttime a good time to listen to God?** (Because everything is still and quiet; nothing else is grabbing our attention.)

♦ **When are other times you can listen for God?** (When I'm riding the school bus; when I'm in church; when I'm waiting in line at lunch.)

Say: **Because Samuel was listening, God gave him a big, important job to do. Samuel became the leader of the whole nation of Israel. But it's important to remember Samuel didn't understand what God was doing right at first. He had to turn to an older friend for guidance.**

You may need to do that, too. God doesn't often speak to people in an out-loud voice. Sometimes, he speaks to us more silently, and we may need to ask other people for help in deciding whether it's really God talking to us. Ask:

♦ **Who are some people who could help you understand when God is talking to you?** (Parents; the pastor; Sunday school teachers.)

Say: **God has wonderful things in store for people who are willing to listen to him and to obey, and it doesn't make any difference if you're young, old, or in between!** ★ **It's important to listen to God!**

Need to talk about

Teacher Tip

Seat yourself among the kids in the middle. Being in the middle of a group of kids instead of in front of them helps you keep control and their attention in a storytelling situation.

LIFE APPLICATION

All the Good Things

Say: **Speaking of listening, I know you're all experts in commercials. How many commercials would you guess you see on television in one week?** Allow kids to guess. **Now's your chance to make a commercial about something really important.**

Form two groups. Have one group plan a commercial about the good things that come from reading the Bible. Have the other group plan a commercial about the benefits of listening to God. Appoint a director for each group. Encourage the directors to plan commercials where the younger kids can play an important part.

Allow time for the groups to plan and rehearse their commercials. Then have them perform for each other.

COMMITMENT

Time With God

Say: ★ **It's important to listen to God, and I'm glad you're all excited about looking for God's guidance. I have a little journal for each of you that will help you keep praying and reading your Bible each day.**

Give kids each a photocopy of the "I'm Listening, Lord" mini-journal and a pencil. Show kids how to fold the journal, and help younger kids write their names on the front.

Explain that the journal has a place where kids can write each day what they read, what they prayed about and what they thought about after reading the Bible and praying.

Explain to kids who don't yet have reading and writing skills that they can look at a Bible-story book each day and draw pictures of the Bible story in their journals. They can also draw pictures of the things they pray about and of how they feel after being quiet with God for a while.

Ask:

♦ **When would be a good time for you to have your quiet time with God each day?** Ask kids to respond individually, and then fill in the hands of the clock to show the time they named. Encourage kids to think of this time as an appointment with someone who loves them very much.

LESSON AIM

To help kids understand that ★ God is more powerful than anything or anybody.

OBJECTIVES

Kids will
✓ be challenged to do difficult tasks,
✓ participate in a lopsided tug of war,
✓ celebrate Gideon's victory, and
✓ make a commitment to rely on God's power.

YOU'LL NEED

❏ 3 lunch bags
❏ 2 large safety pins
❏ 3 balloons
❏ 2 bananas*
❏ a plastic knife
❏ several self-adhesive bandages
❏ transparent tape
❏ star stickers
❏ several feet of rope
❏ scissors
❏ straight pins
❏ ribbon
❏ photocopies of the "Power Pinwheel" handout (p. 74)
❏ plastic drinking straws
❏ a hole punch
❏ a large electric fan
*Always check for allergies before serving snacks.

all-in-one
SUNDAY
SCHOOL

BIBLE BASIS

Judges 6:1–7:23

Gideon's story begins with a sad tale of oppression. The Israelites lived in fear of their stronger Midianite neighbors, who had a nasty habit of swooping down at harvest time to plunder and ruin the Israelites' crops. Judges 6:5 says the Midianite invaders covered the land like swarms of locusts. God's people were left in such poverty by these systematic attacks that they cried to the Lord for help. God chose Gideon for the job.

Gideon is a hero after my own heart. An angel found him threshing wheat under cover of a wine press, hoping to save his meager harvest from invaders. The angel hailed Gideon, saying, "The Lord is with you, mighty warrior!" Excuse me—a warrior in a wine press? Just so! God was about to put in motion a most unlikely series of events that would free Israel from the Midianite threat, make Gideon a national hero, and restore the hearts of a wayward people. Sometimes, perhaps just to remind us where the real power lies, God chooses to use a meek man rather than a muscleman!

2 Corinthians 12:9b-10

"When I am weak, then I am strong." This is the sort of paradox that makes non-Christians scratch their heads and stare. But what a glorious fact for those who believe! When we're drained and in over our heads, we throw ourselves on God's mercy. That's when miraculous things begin to happen.

UNDERSTANDING YOUR KIDS

Overwhelmed. That's the perfect word to describe today's kids. Both parents and kids are guilty of cramming life so full that there's barely time to stop and take a deep breath. Why? Nobody wants to miss out. Little League, after all, lasts only a few years. And if kids don't start gymnastics (music lessons, soccer, ballet, football) early, they'll never be competitive. Kids who aren't on the go as much as their neighbors tend to feel second-rate. And we adults certainly don't want our kids to miss any of the memorable experiences of childhood! For most kids today, the pressure never lets up. They might welcome the idea of hiding in a wine press!

Your kids will love meeting Gideon. They'll laugh at his deplorably low self-esteem. They'll gasp when God whittles down his army. And they'll cheer when the 90-pound weakling with God's power in his afterburners chases the bad guys all the way across the river. This story is good news for kids who are so maxed out that it's an act of heroism just to get up in the morning.

ATTENTION GRABBER

Triple Challenge

Before class, gather three lunch bags. In bag one, place three uninflated balloons and a large safety pin. In bag two, place two unpeeled bananas and a plastic knife. Place several adhesive bandages in bag three. Place a roll of transparent tape and another large safety pin in a conspicuous place in the room.

Put star stickers on kids as they arrive. Put a sticker on the cheek of the first person, on the hand of the second person, and on the nose of the third person. Continue in this manner so that one-third of the group has cheek stickers, one-third has hand stickers, and one-third has nose stickers. Keep a balance of younger and older kids in each group.

After everyone has arrived, say: **Welcome to our Triple Challenge! I can see that you're all stars, so you shouldn't have any trouble meeting my challenges! To get started, I'd like you to form three groups—the Cheeks, the Hands, and the Noses. All the people with hand stickers meet over there, people with cheek stickers meet over there, and people with nose stickers meet over there.**

When groups have gathered, take bag one to the Cheeks and say: **Your challenge is to poke a pin into an inflated balloon without popping the balloon.** Take bag two to the Hands and say: **Your challenge is to slice an unpeeled banana without slicing the skin of the banana.** Take bag three to the Noses and say: **Your challenge is to stick out your tongue and touch your nose. As you're all practicing, please be careful not to injure yourselves.**

You have your supplies. If you see anything else in the room that might help you, feel free to use it. You'll have three minutes to accomplish your challenge. I'm sorry, but I can't answer any questions during the three minutes. Go!

If kids approach you with questions, steadfastly refuse to answer. After three minutes (or earlier if one group seems inclined to give up), call time and ask each group to report. Applaud any group that accomplished its challenge. To groups that couldn't accomplish their challenges, say: **You know, the challenges I gave you are easier than they seem.**

Demonstrate how to meet each challenge. Before sticking a pin into an inflated balloon, place a piece of transparent tape over the place where you'll insert the pin. To slice an unpeeled banana without slicing its skin, poke a pin into the banana at one-inch intervals and wiggle the pin back and forth. When you peel the banana—voilà! It's already sliced. To stick out your tongue and touch your nose, stick out your tongue and then touch your nose with a finger.

Say: **See? That wasn't so hard!** Ask:

♦ **What was it like when I gave you your challenge?** (Like I could never do that.)

♦ **What went through your mind when I showed you how simple it is to accomplish each challenge?** (I couldn't believe it; I was amazed.)

Say: **Our Bible story today is about a man who felt a lot like you did when I first presented the challenges. Let's find out what his challenge was and how this man found out that ★ God is more powerful than anything or anybody.**

BIBLE STUDY

Lopsided War (Judges 6:1–7:23)

Hold up a rope and say: **I'd like to begin our Bible story with a game of Tug of War. Who would like to play?** Choose several of the smallest volunteers to form one team and several bigger kids to form the other team. Have the teams take positions on either end of the rope. Ask:

♦ **How might this match turn out?** (The big kids will win.)

Say: **Ready, set—oops! I almost forgot something.** Point to the first member of the smaller team and say: **I think you can handle this job by yourself. I'd like the rest of the people on your team to drop the rope and sit down.** Now there should be one small child facing several bigger children.

Say: **Good! That's better. I like the way this game is shaping up.** Ask:

♦ **Given the way the contest is set up right now, what are the chances that** [name of smaller child] **will win?** (Almost none; not unless a miracle happens.)

Say: **This is how it was when the hero of our Bible story went to war. The odds didn't look good at all. Let's see what happened. First I'll need someone to be Gideon.** Choose a volunteer. **Now I'll need an angel.** Choose a second volunteer. **You bigger kids will be the Midianites. Choose a captain for your team. You smaller kids will be the Israelites. Gideon will be the captain of your team.**

Have the teams stand facing each other. Have Gideon and the angel stand beside you. Put the rope away so that it won't distract the children as they act out the Bible story.

Say: **As I read the Bible story, the captains will show or tell you how to act it out. Gideon, in addition to being the captain of your team, you'll act out what Gideon does.**

THE "WHO, ME?" HERO

(based on Judges 6:1–7:23)

It was a dark time in the nation of Israel. The Israelites never knew when powerful Midianite soldiers would ride in on camels to kill people, steal their livestock, and ruin or steal their crops. There were so many enemy soldiers that it was hopeless for the Israelites to even try to fight back. Seven years of constant raids left the Israelites poor and starving. Finally they cried out to God for help.

God had a plan. The plan involved a young Israelite named Gideon. Gideon was an ordinary young man who was just as afraid of the Midianites as anyone else. In fact, he was threshing his wheat in a wine press, hoping that Midianite soldiers wouldn't find him there.

Suddenly an angel appeared to Gideon and said, "The Lord is with you, mighty warrior!"

Gideon asked, "If the Lord is with us, why are we having so much trouble with the Midianites?"

The Lord said, "Go with the strength you have and save Israel. I am sending you."

"But, Lord," Gideon answered, "how can I save Israel? I belong to the smallest family of one of the weakest tribes, and I'm the least important member of my family!"

The Lord said, "I will be with you, and you will strike down the Midianites!"

Gideon replied, "If you're really pleased with me, give me proof. Please wait here until I bring you an offering."

The angel agreed to wait, so Gideon hurried to prepare a meal and placed it on a rock near where the angel was sitting. The angel touched the food with the tip of his staff, and fire jumped out of the rock and completely burned up the food! Then the angel disappeared.

"I've seen the angel of the Lord face to face!" Gideon exclaimed. Then he built an altar and worshipped God.

Some time later, the Midianites and their allies massed their troops to form a huge army of well over 100,000 men. They camped in a valley, waiting for just the right moment to attack Israel. When Gideon heard of this threat, God's Spirit came upon him. Gideon blew his trumpet and called for the fighting men of Israel to join him. Gideon led Israel's army to a valley south of the Midianite army. Both camps prepared for battle.

Then the Lord said to Gideon, "You have too many men! I don't want your soldiers to brag that they defeated the Midianites by their own strength. Tell any soldier who is afraid that he can go home." Gideon did as the Lord said, and 22,000 men went home, leaving Gideon only 10,000 soldiers.

Then the Lord said to Gideon, "There are still too many men. Take them down to the water for a drink. Send home any man who gets down on his knees to drink."

Gideon did just as the Lord commanded. Almost all the men got down on their knees to drink. Gideon sent them home. That left him with *only 300 soldiers!*

God said, "With these 300 men I'll save you and help you defeat the Midianites." Gideon trusted God and prepared to go into battle with only 300 men.

In the middle of the night, God told Gideon to take his servant and sneak into the enemy camp, where most of the soldiers were resting in their tents. Gideon climbed down to the valley and tiptoed to the edge of the Midianite camp. It was *huge!* There were more soldiers and camels than anyone could count. What could his little army of 300 men do against more than 100,000 soldiers?

(continued)

Gideon and his servant crept so close to an enemy tent that they could hear the soldiers talking. One soldier was telling another that he'd dreamed that a loaf of bread rolled into the camp and knocked the tent over flat. The other soldier said, "Your dream is about the sword of Gideon. God will use him to defeat our whole army!"

Gideon and his servant scurried back to their own camp. "Get up!" Gideon ordered. "The Lord has handed the army of Midian over to you!"

Gideon made sure each of his soldiers had a trumpet and a clay jar with a burning torch inside it. Under cover of darkness, Gideon's 300 men quietly surrounded the enemy camp. On Gideon's signal, each man blew his trumpet and shouted, "For the Lord and for Gideon!" Then they smashed their clay jars and let the torches burn brightly.

The sneak attack threw the enemy camp into a panic. The enemy soldiers began fighting each other. Then Gideon and his men chased them far from the land, and God's people lived in peace for many years.

Angel, listen carefully for your part and be ready to act out what you hear. Okay, troops, we're about to go into battle, so pay careful attention to what your captains say and do.

Read "The 'Who, Me?' Hero" script. Use lots of drama in your reading. Keep an eye on the captains and offer suggestions for directing their teams to act out the story.

Finish with a hearty round of applause. Then ask:

♦ **How was this Bible story like the tug of war we set up earlier?** (One side was much stronger; the odds seemed hopeless.)

♦ **Why do you think the Lord kept telling Gideon to send men home?** (Because he wanted to see if Gideon trusted him; God wanted to use his own power to defeat the Midianites.)

♦ **Why did God choose an ordinary man like Gideon to lead his people?** (Because an ordinary man would have to trust God; because God didn't need a powerful leader.)

♦ **What would you have thought of Gideon's plan if you had been one of the 300 soldiers who stayed to fight?** (I'd have thought he was nuts; I'd want to go home, too.)

♦ **How is God just as powerful today as he was in Gideon's day?** (God never changes.)

Say: **God took an ordinary, frightened young man and turned him into a hero. God used an army of 300 men to defeat an enemy with more than 100,000 soldiers. The night of that battle, God's people learned that ★ God is more powerful than anything or anybody. And God never changes. God can help us today just as he helped Gideon long ago.**

LIFE APPLICATION

Scary Stuff

Have kids arrange chairs in a semicircle and sit facing you.

Say: **Gideon was hiding, and he was scared to death. Let's learn a rap that reminds us of how God changed Gideon from a scaredy-cat to a hero. Here's how the first part of the rap goes. I'll say a line and then you repeat it after me.**

Standin' in a wine press (*cross fists over heart*)**,**
Shaking with fear (*shake all over*)**,**
Hope there's no enemy (*cup hands around eyes; look around*)
Sneakin' round here. (*Tiptoe in place.*)

Repeat the rap once or twice until kids are comfortable with the words and actions.

Then say: **I don't know about you, but there have been plenty of times in my life when I felt scared, outnumbered, and ready to run in the other direction, just like Gideon. All of us get scared by different things. I'm going to read a list of scary things. If what I read wouldn't scare you at all, stay seated. If it would scare you a little bit, stand up. If it would scare you a whole lot, stand up and wave your arms over your head. When I read something really scary, I should feel a breeze from all the arms waving. Let's do our rap once more as a reminder of how scared Gideon was at the beginning of the story.**

Standin' in a wine press (*cross fists over heart*)**,**
Shaking with fear (*shake all over*)**,**
Hope there's no enemy (*cup hands around eyes; look around*)
Sneakin' round here. (*Tiptoe in place.*)

Read the following list, pausing after each item for kids to respond. Say: **Show how you would feel...**

♦ **just before a math test.**
♦ **when you have to play an instrument or sing in front of lots of people.**
♦ **when your family's car breaks down on a long trip.**
♦ **during a spelling bee.**
♦ **when a gang of kids makes fun of you on the playground.**
♦ **when you have to give an oral report.**
♦ **when you're home alone at night.**
♦ **when a parent is having trouble at work.**
♦ **when you wake up with a bad dream.**
♦ **when you are called to the principal's office.**
♦ **when there's a really bad storm and the lights go out.**
Ask:
♦ **Does anyone want to tell about another time you felt really scared?** Allow children to share.

Say: **That's all pretty scary stuff. We know that Gideon was scared at the beginning of the story.** Ask:

♦ **What changed Gideon from a scaredy-cat to a hero?** (God did; God sent an angel to him; God let him hear how scared the enemy soldiers were.)

Say: **There's a verse in the New Testament that helps us understand what happened to Gideon. Listen to 2 Corinthians 12:10: "That's why I take pleasure in my weaknesses, and in the insults, hardships, persecutions, and troubles that I suffer for Christ. For when I am weak, then I am strong."** Ask:

♦ **What kinds of insults and hard times did Gideon face?** (Enemies stole his crops; he was afraid of being invaded; he had to hide his food from enemy soldiers.)

♦ **How did Gideon discover that when he was weak, then he was truly strong?** (When he couldn't do anything, God took over; he learned to trust God's power.)

♦ **What does "when I am weak, then I am strong" mean to you?** (That I can do anything with God's power; that I'm strong when I let God take over.)

Say: **Let's learn the second part of the Gideon rap. This part tells about Gideon, the hero.** Teach kids this rap line by line; repeat it once or twice until they're comfortable with it.

Look at all our enemies *(point)*
Shakin' with fear. *(Shake all over.)*
When this battle's over, they'll know *(make fists)*
God was here! *(Shake finger and point to the sky.)*

Say: **We can look to God for strength just as Gideon did. God's not looking for musclemen and heroes. God's looking for ordinary people who believe that ★ God is more powerful than anything or anybody.**

COMMITMENT

Power Pinwheels

Set out scissors, transparent tape, straight pins, 18-inch lengths of ribbon, photocopies of the "Power Pinwheel" handout, plastic drinking straws, and a hole punch. Before kids begin to work, point out Ephesians 6:10 at the top of the handout and read it aloud. Then ask kids to read it aloud with you. (Have young nonreaders join in after they've heard it repeated.)

Say: **Think of all the different ways you can be strong in the Lord. When you've thought of a way, stand up and make a muscle, like this.** Flex your biceps.

Kids might mention ways such as reading the Bible, praying, tuning in to God's plan, asking others to pray with them, counting on God's strength instead of their own, and trusting God even when they're scared. Ask:

♦ **What gives power to turn a pinwheel?** (The wind.)

♦ **Where does the wind come from?** (The weather; from God.)

Say: **These pinwheels will remind us to count on God's power, not on our own.**

Have kids work in "power pairs" to make their pinwheels. Have each child find a partner who was on the opposite team during the Bible story. As children finish, challenge them to blow on their pinwheels to see how quickly and steadily they can make their pinwheels turn.

Then set a large electric fan on a table and turn it on high. Let the kids hold up their pinwheels to catch the wind from the fan. After a few moments, stop the fan and ask:

♦ **How was the wind from the fan like God's power?** (It's stronger than our own power; it does more than we could ever do.)

Say: ★ **God is more powerful than anything or anybody. Turn to your partner and tell one way you'll rely on God's power this week.**

Allow a minute or two for partners to share. Then call everyone together and ask kids to tell what their partners said they would do to rely on God's power.

Teacher Tip

Make your own Power Pinwheel before class so you'll be familiar with the process. To make really dazzling pinwheels, purchase holographic wrapping paper. Let students use the handout as a pattern to cut their pinwheels from the sparkling paper.

CLOSING

Blown Away

After everyone has shared, gather kids in a circle and have them raise their Power Pinwheels high. Close with a prayer similar to this one: **Dear Lord, sometimes your power blows us away! You helped Gideon change from a scaredy-cat to a hero. You defeated a huge army with only 300 men. Help us to remember that ★ you're more powerful than anything or anybody and that we can rely on your power when we face scary things. In Jesus' name, amen.**

POWER PINWHEEL

"Be strong in the Lord and in his mighty power" (Ephesians 6:10).

1 Cut out the square; then cut in on the diagonal lines. (Be sure not to cut all the way to the center.)

2 Fold two opposing corners marked with arrows to the center and secure them with a tiny piece of transparent tape.

3 Do the same with the other two corners.

4 Push a straight pin through the center of the pinwheel and into one end of a plastic drinking straw.

5 Experiment and adjust the pin so the pinwheel moves freely but doesn't flop around.

6 Pinch the other end of the straw and make a hole in it with a hole punch. Thread and tie several lengths of ribbon through the hole.

BE
STRONG
LORD
IN THE

Faith to Give Away

LESSON AIM

To help kids understand that ★ it's important to tell others about God's love.

OBJECTIVES

Kids will

✓ learn how Naaman's servant girl told about God's prophet,

✓ explore the treasures God offers those who believe in Jesus, and

✓ commit to caring for people by looking for opportunities to share their faith.

YOU'LL NEED

❑ bubbles and a bubble wand
❑ a noisemaker
❑ Bibles
❑ a photocopy of the "Bible-Story Name Tags" handout (p. 81)
❑ scissors
❑ safety pins
❑ a gift-wrapped box of bubble gum*
❑ photocopies of the "Treasure Slips" handout (p. 82)
❑ aluminum foil
❑ ribbon

*Always check for allergies before serving snacks.

BIBLE BASIS

2 Kings 5:1-17

This is a touching story of faith and devotion from an unexpected source. Foreign soldiers kidnap a Hebrew girl in a raid, then carry her off to work in the home of the army's commander.

You'd think the child would be sullen and rebellious—ready to escape or sabotage her captors at the first opportunity. But, amazingly, this nameless girl cares for her master and urges him to go to Elisha for a cure for leprosy. Talk about loving your enemies!

We often think of sharing our faith as orally explaining God's plan of redemption. But let's not put such a crucial element of our faith life in such a small box. The girl in the story witnessed by caring about her master's illness and expressing her faith that God's prophet could heal him. This is the key: We share our faith in any number of ways because we truly care about people and want to point them to the living God.

Romans 10:14-15

It doesn't require a seminary degree to share with others the good news that Jesus offers us forgiveness and the opportunity to become children of God. The news we have to share is good news! Let's not keep it to ourselves!

UNDERSTANDING YOUR KIDS

Did you ever try to shut down a group of kids who were really excited about something? It's close to impossible! That's what makes kids so great. They're sincere and transparent and full of energy. So when they get excited about their walk with God, watch out! Great things will happen.

How do you get them excited? Let them see how God works in people's lives. Keep them in touch with the prayer life of your church. Involve them in faith-building activities in which they can make a difference, such as a workday at the home of an elderly friend or a visit to an interfaith community-service center. Let kids come face to face with people whose lives are being changed by God's power.

Use this lesson to help kids see that they can make a difference in people's lives by sharing their faith both orally and in creative, practical ways.

ATTENTION GRABBER

Sob Tag

Choose one person to be "It" and another person to be the "healer." Give the healer a bottle of bubbles and a bubble wand.

Say: **We're going to start today with a new game called Sob Tag. If It tags you, you have to kneel down and start crying and sobbing. The only way you can stop sobbing is if the healer blows bubbles over your head. One more thing—no one can run in this game. Everyone moves around the room by taking giant steps, the biggest steps you can possibly take. Let's all practice sobbing before we get started.**

Demonstrate crying and sobbing for the kids. Then say: **Great! You guys sound really sad. Let's play. Remember—no running. Ready to begin? Go!**

Every minute or so shake a noisemaker and allow different children to take the roles of It and the healer. Before kids begin to tire, stop the game with the noisemaker; then have kids take three deep breaths and sit down. Set the bubbles out of sight. Ask:

♦ **What was fun about this game?** (It was different playing Tag with giant steps; it sounded funny with everybody sobbing; it was fun to get bubbles blown on me.)

♦ **What was it like to sob and sob?** (I got tired of it; it was hard not to laugh.)

♦ **When do people cry like that in real life?** (When they've had an accident; when something terrible happens.)

♦ **What was it like to be the healer?** (I wanted to hurry and get to everyone; it was hard to keep ahead of It.)

Say: **In our Bible story we'll find out about a prophet who had special healing power from God. He didn't need bubbles! But the real hero in the story is a bit of a surprise. Listen carefully and, at the end of the story, tell me who you think the hero is. Here's a hint: ★ It's important to tell others about God's love.**

BIBLE STUDY

✴ A Little Girl Who Cared (2 Kings 5:1-17)

Read this Bible story straight from an easy-to-understand version of the Bible. Photocopy the "Bible-Story Name Tags" handout and cut apart the name tags for the characters in the story. Assign the roles by pinning a name tag on the child who will read that character's part. Then be prepared to cue the readers when their parts come up in the text.

Have the characters sit in a semicircle in front of the class with the rest of the children facing them.

Say to the kids who don't have a part: **You have two things to do. This story is about a man named Naaman who was a great general, so each time you hear his name, say, "Yes, sir!"**

Practice the name and response with the kids.

Then say: **Good job. Now you have one more thing to do. This story has two kings in it. Each time you hear the word** *king*, **say, "May you live forever!" That's what people said in Old Testament times to show respect. Let's try that. King!** (Pause as kids respond.) **Great! Now let's get on with the story. Don't forget to listen for who the real hero is. Narrator, you're on!**

Finish the story with a big round of applause. Then ask:

♦ Okay—who would you say is the hero of this story? Accept all answers and have kids tell why they chose a particular character.

Say: **My choice for the hero of this story is the little servant girl.**

♦ **Why do you think I chose her?** (Because she told her master about Elisha; because she cared for people even though she was a slave.)

Say: **I don't know about you, but if I got kidnapped from my home and was forced to work in another family, I think I might be a little unfriendly to the people I had to work for.**

Ask:

♦ **Why do you think this little servant girl wanted to help her master?** (She was a kind, loving person; maybe her master's family was nice to her; she believed in God and wanted others to believe in God, too.)

Say: **Isn't it interesting that we don't even know the little girl's name? But what we do know about her is pretty important. She cared enough about her master to tell him what God's prophet could do. And ★ it's important to tell others about God's love.**

Teacher Tip

If some characters have trouble with their parts, consider reading through the story a second time.

LIFE APPLICATION

Bub-Bub-Bub-Bubblin'!

Different Candy

Put enough bubble gum in a box for each child to have two or three pieces. Gift-wrap the box and place it where children will see it and wonder about it.

Pick up the box and say: **Hmm. I think I've kept you in suspense long enough. It's about time to give this away. I wonder who'll catch it.** Turn your back to the children and toss the

78

box over your shoulder. If more than one child grabs for the box, say: **Don't worry—I think there'll be plenty for everyone.**

Invite the child who caught the box to open it. Let everyone peek inside. Then have the child who opened the box help you toss pieces of bubble gum to everyone. Put a piece of bubble gum in your mouth and say: **I wonder if anyone can blow a bubble faster than I can!**

Have kids gather in a circle as they all blow bubbles. Then say: **Let's all blow one more bubble together. Then when I pop my bubble, you pop yours, too.**

After all the bubbles have popped, ask:

♦ **How was what** [name of the child who caught the box] **did like what the little girl in the Bible story did?** (He shared the good thing with others; she didn't keep the good thing to herself.)

♦ **What would've happened if the little girl in the story hadn't told her master about what God could do?** (He would've died; he would've been in pain for the rest of his life.)

♦ **What would've happened if** [name of child] **had kept all the bubble gum?** (I would've been sad; I would've asked for some.)

♦ **How is that like what happens if we don't tell others about God's love?** (They are left out; they don't know about God's forgiveness and the other good things they're missing.)

Have a volunteer look up and read Romans 10:14-15. Ask:

♦ **What does this verse mean to you?** (People need a chance to hear about God before they can believe; people can't believe in God if they've never heard of him.)

Say: **Having Jesus in our lives makes us so happy that we want to share it with everyone. We just bubble over! Quickly find a partner and blow bubbles together. Then pop your bubbles and tell each other the name of one person you want to share God's love with this week. Ready? Set? Blow!**

COMMITMENT

Hidden Treasure

Before class, photocopy the "Treasure Slips" handout, cut the slips apart, and wrap them in aluminum foil in the shape of Hershey's Kisses chocolates. Use ribbon to tie a small bow around the neck of each one, and then hide the "treasures" around the room.

Shake the noisemaker to bring everyone together. Ask:

♦ **What good thing happened to Naaman after he heard about the true God?** (He was healed.)

Say: **Do you know that something even better than that**

Teacher Tip

If you have a child who isn't allowed to chew gum, give him or her a balloon to blow up instead. Rather than popping the balloon in the following activities, have the child let the balloon deflate. Dispose of any broken balloon pieces promptly, as they can present a choking hazard.

happens to everyone who hears about Jesus and believes in him? A whole bunch of really good things happen. I've hidden some of those things around the room. There are seven hidden treasures for you to find. Nobody can claim more than one. When you find a treasure, bring it to me. When you've found all seven treasures, we'll open them together.

Let the children open and read the treasures. If a nonreader finds a treasure, let him or her choose an older child to read it to the class.

After all seven treasure slips have been read aloud, say:

★ It's important to tell others about God's love—starting with your very own family. So let's make treasures you can share with your family this week—one treasure slip per day.

Distribute scissors, pieces of aluminum foil, and photocopies of the "Treasure Slips" handout. Have kids cut apart the treasure slips. As they're cutting, place another piece of bubble gum beside each person.

Say: Put the bubble gum in the center of your foil. Then twist the foil around the treasure slips in the shape of a big Hershey's Kisses chocolate. You can put your treasure on your table at home. Each night, have someone in your family pull out a treasure slip. Then look up the Bible verse and read it together. On the last night, pull out the bubble gum and tell how you bubbled over telling others about God's love during the week.

Teacher Tip

If you have time, have volunteers look up and read the verses referred to on the treasure slips.

CLOSING

Treasure Circle

Have kids stand in a circle holding their treasures.

Pray: Dear Lord, thank you for all these treasures you give us when we believe in you. We know ★ it's important to tell others about God's love. Help us bubble over and share your wonderful treasures with others this week. In Jesus' name, amen.

BIBLE-STORY NAME TAGS

Narrator

Servant Girl

King of Aram

King of Israel

Elisha

Messenger

Naaman

Naaman's Servant

TREASURE SLIPS

God forgives your sins and makes you a new person.

Look up 2 Corinthians 5:17.

God watches over you and hears your prayers.

Look up Philippians 4:6-7.

You become a child of God.

Look up John 1:12.

God gives you Christian friends who love you and help you grow.

Look up 1 John 3:16-18.

Jesus gives you peace and helps you be more like him.

Look up John 14:27.

Jesus takes you to heaven where you'll live forever with him.

Look up John 14:1-3.

God gives you all the wonderful promises in the Bible.

Look up Psalm 145:13.

LESSON AIM

To help kids understand that ★ God helps us stand up for what's right.

OBJECTIVES

Kids will

✓ play a mismatched game,
✓ learn how God helped Shadrach, Meshach, and Abednego when they stood up for what was right,
✓ develop responses to situations involving peer pressure, and
✓ affirm each other's commitment to doing what's right.

YOU'LL NEED

❑ masking tape *Church*
❑ table tennis balls *Church*
❑ a whistle
❑ a photocopy of the "Statue and the Fourth Man" figures (p. 92)
❑ photocopies of the "Three Men and the Flames" figures (p. 93)
❑ gold paper or shiny gold gift wrap
❑ scissors
❑ beige paper
❑ red paper
❑ a Bible
❑ a photocopy of the "Hot Spots" cards (p. 94)

BIBLE BASIS

Daniel 3:1-30

When our kids were little, we would say, "Hot! Hot! Hot!" to warn them away from objects that might burn them. King Nebuchadnezzar made it very clear to Shadrach, Meshach,

all-in-one
SUNDAY
SCHOOL

and Abednego just how "Hot! Hot! Hot!" things would get if they didn't bow before his massive golden statue. But in the face of royal wrath, the three Hebrew heroes kept their cool. "The God we serve is able to save us from the furnace" seemed clear enough to inform the king of their intention to disobey. But then they added, "But even if God does not save us, we want you, O king, to know this: We will not serve your gods or worship the gold statue you have set up." Wowie zowie! No careful diplomacy here. These guys were ready and willing to take the heat.

Where did this holy audacity come from? Absolute faith in the fact that "the Lord our God, the Lord is one" and that the gold statue was nothing more than a pathetic imitation—a gaudy symbol of a king's pride. So when the king pulled a power play, the three valiant Hebrews stood their ground. Their courage and God's miraculous deliverance changed a king's heart and taught a pagan empire to humble itself before the true God. Today, as in ancient times, courage is born of absolute confidence in the power of God and the truth of his Word. Because we can't see God with human eyes, we sometimes let ourselves be intimidated by the flames. But God hasn't changed. When we stand up for what's right, there's a great, big, omnipotent God right behind us, in front of us, and all around us.

Matthew 7:13-14

Jesus tells us that a broad road leads to destruction and that a narrow road leads to life. This statement helps us understand why we Christians seem to be swimming upstream most of our lives, struggling against a culture that proclaims our beliefs unenlightened and narrow-minded. Let's prepare our kids to swim against the current!

UNDERSTANDING YOUR KIDS

As you approach this lesson on peer pressure, it's important to be familiar with the varying backgrounds of the kids in your class. Some may be home-schooled and largely sheltered from peer pressure. Some may attend Christian schools where pressure to get involved in negative behaviors may be somewhat less than in public schools but is by no means nonexistent. Kids who attend public schools may feel like veterans of peer-pressure battles even in the early grades. Encourage kids to learn what school life is like for others, without passing judgment. This can be a divisive issue among Christians. The safest position to take is one of mutual understanding and respect.

All kids will face peer pressure someday, and it's never too soon to prepare. Use this lesson to help kids see that God will be with them when they stand up for what's right and that they never need to be embarrassed to take a stand for Christ.

The Lesson

ATTENTION GRABBER

Blown Away

Before class divide an open area of your classroom in half by placing a line of masking tape on the floor. Then put down two more lines, one foot to each side of the first. Set four table tennis balls on the middle line.

As kids arrive, have them count off by fours. Have the Ones, Twos, and Threes line up on one side of the room. Have the Fours line up on the other side.

Say: **Let's play a game to discover who the real windbags in our class are. I've placed four table tennis balls on the center line. The lines on either side of the center are the safety lines. Your job is to try to blow the balls across the other team's safety line. No part of your head or body may cross your safety line. You may blow from any position—sitting, squatting, or lying on your stomach. When a ball gets past your safety line, the other team gets a point. When I blow the whistle, we'll place all the balls on the center line and start another round. Ready, set, blow!**

If the Fours protest that their team is much smaller than the other, tell them not to worry and that everything will turn out right.

Blow the whistle as soon as all the table tennis balls are blown past the safety lines. Then reset the balls and begin another round. Ignore the protests of the Fours and continue play for three or four rounds. Then collect the balls and gather everyone in a circle. Ask:

♦ **Were you surprised at how lopsided the score turned out to be?** (No, because one team had so many more players; yes, because the smaller team did okay with so few players.)

Ask the Ones, Twos, and Threes:

♦ **What was it like being on the larger team?** (Cool, because we got the most points; fun, because we didn't have to work as hard; not so fun, because I felt sorry for the people on the other team.)

Ask the Fours:

♦ **What was it like being on your team?** (Discouraging, because we were so outnumbered; fun, because we worked well together.)

♦ **If we played this again, explain which team would you choose to be on.** (The bigger one, because we would win; the smaller one, because it's more of a challenge.)

♦ **How was being on the smaller team like being a**

Color
prayer
Game
Story
Snack

85

Christian in your school or neighborhood? (We're outnumbered; it feels as if there are a lot of people against us; it's not, because I go to a Christian school.)

♦ **Tell about a time you felt really outnumbered because you're a Christian.** Allow two or three kids to share.

Say: **Today we're going to learn that ★ God helps us stand up for what's right. That's pretty easy when we're surrounded by a lot of Christian friends. Then we're on the bigger team. But it can be hard when there are only a few Christians. Then we might feel outnumbered and blown away, just as the smaller team in our game did. But whether we're many or few, ★ God helps us stand up for what's right.**

Our Bible story today is about three young men who stood up for what was right when they were completely outnumbered—and it could have cost them their lives.

BIBLE STUDY

The Fiery Furnace (based on Daniel 3:1-30)

Before class photocopy the "Statue and the Fourth Man" figures onto gold paper or trace them on shiny gold gift wrap. Cut the two figures apart on line 1.

Copy the "Three Men and the Flames" figure onto beige paper. Lay a sheet of red paper under the beige paper. When you cut out the three men, only the beige paper will show. When you cut out and fold up the fire, the flames will be red.

Set the scissors and the photocopied figures beside you. Say: **Long ago in the land of Babylon, there lived a great king named Nebuchadnezzar. King Nebuchadnezzar decided to make a huge statue.**

Fold the statue figure in half on line 2. (See diagram 1.)

We're talkin' really huge—as tall as 15 tall basketball players standing on top of each other's shoulders! The king had this giant statue covered with pure gold.

Cut the statue figure from A to B.
Imagine how it gleamed in the sun.

Unfold the statue figure (diagram 2).

The king was proud of his statue—so proud, in fact, that he wanted everyone to bow down and worship it. So the king made a rule. Every time the horns, pipes, flutes, and other instruments played, anyone who didn't bow down and worship the statue would be thrown into a fiery furnace.

That was a problem for three men named Shadrach, Meshach, and Abednego.

Fold the beige paper in half on line 1 (diagram 3).

Cut the men from A to B; then cut to the right edge of the paper to remove the top section.

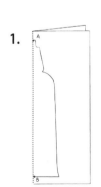

Teacher Tip

Practice cutting and folding the figures before class so you can do it confidently as you tell the story.

1.

86

They were Jews who'd been forced to lived in Babylon after the Babylonian army defeated the army of Judah. Even though they lived in exile, Shadrach, Meshach, and Abednego still worshipped God and obeyed God's Word. God's Word teaches that we should worship only the one, true God. So Shadrach, Meshach, and Abednego weren't about to bow down to the king's gold statue—even if it meant being thrown in a fiery furnace.

Fold the three men again, this time on line 2. Cut out and remove section 3.

2.

But everyone else in Babylon did exactly what the king had ordered. When the horns, pipes, flutes, and other instruments played, they bowed down. But Shadrach, Meshach, and Abednego stood straight up.

Unfold the figure of the three men and hold it up (diagram 4).

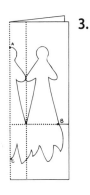

3.

As you can imagine, there were nasty people who just couldn't wait to tell King Nebuchadnezzar about the three Jews who stood straight up when everyone else bowed down. When the king heard about them, he was furious.

"Bring those men to me!" he shouted. So Shadrach, Meshach, and Abednego came before the king.

"Is it true that you do not serve my gods or bow down to my golden statue?" he demanded. "I'll give you one more chance. If you bow down the next time the instruments play, everything will be okay. But if you refuse to bow down, you'll be thrown immediately into a blazing furnace. Then what god will rescue you?"

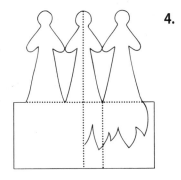

4.

Shadrach, Meshach, and Abednego replied, "If you throw us into the furnace, our God can rescue us. But even if he doesn't, we will not serve your gods or worship your golden statue."

The king flew into a rage. "Heat the furnace seven times hotter than usual!" he ordered. "You soldiers over there—tie these men up and throw them in the fire!"

Fold the three men in half on the middle line (diagram 5). Cut from B to C.

So the soldiers tied up Shadrach, Meshach, and Abednego and pushed them into the furnace. The roaring flames leaped out of the furnace and killed the soldiers.

Unfold the three men and fold up the flames on line 4 so they are in front of the three men (diagram 6).

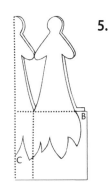

5.

But Shadrach, Meshach, and Abednego weren't hurt at all. In fact, they were walking around inside the furnace.

King Nebuchadnezzar jumped up and stared into the fire, amazed.

Fold the figure of the fourth man in half on line 3 (diagram 7).

6.

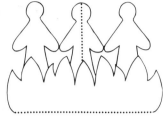

7.

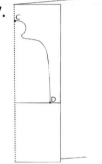

8.

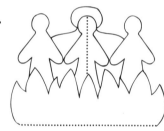

Cut the fourth man from C to D.

"Didn't we throw three men into the fire?" he asked.

Cut off the fourth man figure on line 4. Then hold the fourth man behind the three men in the fire (diagram 8).

"I see four men walking around in there. They're not tied up, and they're not hurt at all! The fourth man looks like a son of the gods!"

Then the king walked right up to the furnace and called out, "Shadrach, Meshach, and Abednego, servants of the Most High God, come out! Come here!"

Shadrach, Meshach, and Abednego came out of the fire. Everyone crowded around in amazement. Their clothes weren't burned; their hair wasn't singed—they didn't even smell of smoke!

Let's read the end of this story straight from the Bible.

Have a good dramatic reader look up and read aloud Daniel 3:28-30.

Then say: **Let's have a round of applause for our three brave men! Now close your eyes for a moment. Think of a furious, raging king standing right in front of you.** Pause for a moment. **Think of a roaring, ravenous fire right behind you.** Pause again. **Now open your eyes.** Ask:

♦ **If you'd been in Shadrach, Meshach, and Abednego's place, what do you think you'd have done?** Allow several kids to respond.

♦ **Do you think they did the right thing? Explain.** (Yes, because they knew it was more important to obey God than to obey the king; yes, because God expects us to obey his Word no matter what.)

♦ **What made Shadrach, Meshach, and Abednego so brave?** (They trusted God's power; they believed God was more powerful than the king.)

♦ **Why do you think God sent a heavenly guardian to protect Shadrach, Meshach, and Abednego?** (Because it would show the king and his officials that only God is the true God; because God loved the three men.)

♦ **What good things happened as a result of the three men standing up for what was right?** (A king believed in God; the whole empire was ordered not to say anything against God.)

Say: **Shadrach, Meshach, and Abednego's brave stand made a huge difference. The proud king learned to honor God and commanded that everyone else in his kingdom respect God. The three men were promoted to more important positions in the government, where they could tell even more people about God. Standing up for what's right isn't always easy, but it can make a huge difference. It may change one person's heart or even a whole kingdom. That's why**
★ **God helps us stand up for what's right.**

LIFE APPLICATION

Hot Spots

Before class photocopy and cut apart the "Hot Spots" cards.

Say: **Not too many people are thrown in fiery furnaces today. But that doesn't mean you don't run into hot spots. I'll show you what I mean.**

Pick up the table tennis balls from the opening activity. As you toss them in the air, say: **Catch these—quick!** Give a "Hot Spots" card to each child who caught a ball.

Say: **Everyone, quickly form a group with the card-holder nearest you. Read the card aloud together and brainstorm what you would do in the situation described on the card. I'll give you one minute to prepare; then each card-holder will report to the class. Go!**

Blow your whistle after one minute. Have card-holders read their cards and tell their groups' responses. Allow the rest of the class to suggest other possible responses. Then collect the used cards and have kids form a cluster in front of you.

Say: **This time when I toss the table tennis balls, stand still with your arms at your sides. The people the balls touch first will be the card-holders for this round.** Toss the balls gently in the air, and give the remainder of the "Hot Spots" cards to the kids touched first by each ball.

Say: **Quickly form groups around the card-holders, just like last time. You'll have one minute to read your cards and come up with responses. Go!**

Call time after one minute and have groups read their cards and give responses. Allow the rest of the kids to suggest other possible responses to each situation. Then collect the cards and ask:

♦ **How was getting the cards like the way you get caught in hot spots in real life?** (Sometimes it's surprising; you never know when it's going to happen; you may try to avoid it, but you can't.)

♦ **Why do Christians often end up in hot spots like these?** (Because we live by God's rules; because we try to obey God and other people don't.)

Say: **Jesus had something interesting to say about going against the crowd.** Have a volunteer read Matthew 7:13-14 aloud. Then ask:

♦ **What do you think Jesus meant when he said that the way that leads to life is narrow?** (He meant that God set a certain path for us to follow; that God's way is different from the way most people go.)

♦ **Why is it that few people choose to go God's way?** (Because they don't want to obey God; because they want to do things their own way.)

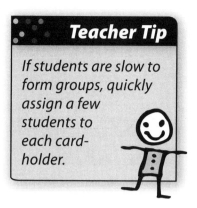

Teacher Tip

If students are slow to form groups, quickly assign a few students to each card-holder.

♦ **How does Jesus' statement help explain why Christians have to battle peer pressure?** (It tells us to expect only a few people to take the narrow way; it tells us that most people will miss the way to life.)

Say: **Jesus told his followers to expect to go against the crowd. But he also said something to encourage us.** Have volunteers read John 14:15-17 and 16:33. Ask:

♦ **How did Jesus overcome the world?** (He died on the cross and then came back to life; he took our sins for us.)

Say: **Before Jesus went back to heaven, he promised to send a helper—the Holy Spirit. When we find ourselves in hot spots, we can say a quick prayer and ask the Holy Spirit to help us. That's one way ★ God helps us stand up for what's right. Let's discover another way we can find courage and help to stand up for what's right.**

COMMITMENT

Rap It Up

Say: **As I read this Scripture passage, listen carefully for four things the writer, Paul, tells Christians to do. Each time you hear one of those four things, wave your hand in the air, and then put it down. Here we go.**

"Only one thing concerns me: Be sure that you live in a way that brings honor to the Good News of Christ. Then... I will hear that you are standing strong with one purpose, that you work together as one for the faith of the Good News, and that you are not afraid of those who are against you" (Philippians 1:27-28a, NCV).

♦ **What does Paul tell Christians to do?** (Live in a way that brings honor to Christ; stand strong with one purpose; work together as one; don't be afraid of those who are against you.)

Say: **When we do all those things, we help each other stand up for what's right. That's called positive peer pressure. Shadrach, Meshach, and Abednego supported each other in their stand against the king. That positive peer pressure helped them do what was right even though it could have cost them their lives. We can influence each other with positive peer pressure too.** Ask:

♦ **Who can tell about a time when having other Christians around helped you do what was right?** Allow two or three kids to share.

Say: **Let's make a reminder of the brave stand Shadrach, Meshach, and Abednego took and of how they helped each other.**

Distribute scissors and photocopies of the "Three Men and the Flames" figures. Lead kids step by step through the folding and cutting sequence from the Bible story. When everyone has cut out a figure, have kids form a circle, and then lead them in reading aloud the rap that's printed on the flames. If you have young nonreaders in your class, go over the words twice and have them repeat each line after you. Then teach kids the motions printed below.

When peer pressure's pushin' (*push forward three times*),
And it's feelin' kinda tight (*crunch arms close to your sides and rock from side to side*),
Just remember that it's cool (*shake a finger; then give someone a high five on "cool"*)
To stand up for what's right! (*Wave arms high; then lets arms rest on the shoulders of people beside you.*)

For extra fun after kids have learned the rap and motions, have them form two lines facing each other. Have one group say the first line, then have the other group say the second line. On the third line, have kids give high fives to people they're facing in the opposite group. On the fourth line, have them step together and rest their arms on each other. (Each child will be facing the opposite direction of the person on either side of him or her.)

Let kids practice the rap several times. Then gather everyone in a circle and say: ★ **God helps us stand up for what's right. One way God helps us is by giving us Christian friends. Right now I'd like you to give a handshake or a high five to all the other kids and say, "I'm gonna' help you do what's right." Let's see how quickly we can all shake hands and say that to each other.**

CLOSING

Pile-of-Hands Prayer

After handshakes and high fives, gather kids in a huddle and have them make a pile of hands in the center. Close with a prayer similar to this one: **Dear Lord, please give us courage to stand up for what's right even when it's hard or scary. Help us to encourage each other. In Jesus' name, amen.**

Line 3

C

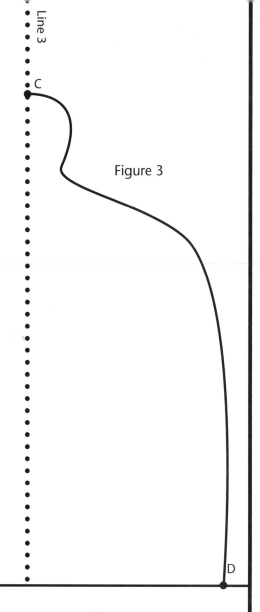

Figure 3

D

Line 4

THE STATUE AND THE FOURTH MAN

Line 1

A

Line 2

Line 2

B

THE THREE MEN AND THE FLAMES

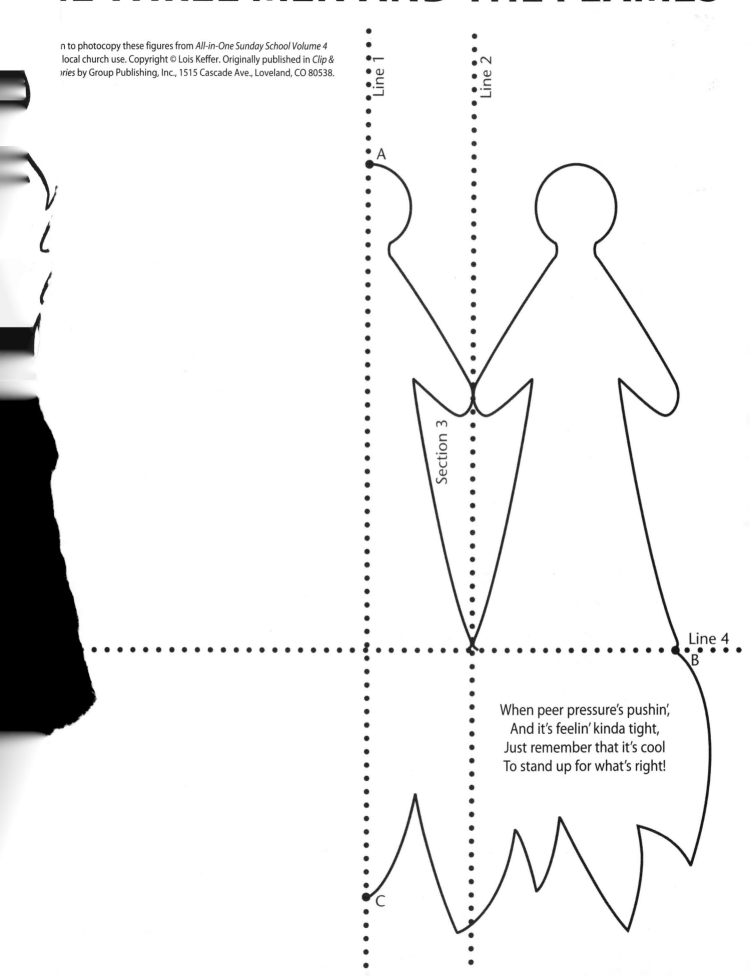

Line 1

Line 2

A

Section 3

Line 4

B

C

When peer pressure's pushin',
And it's feelin' kinda tight,
Just remember that it's cool
To stand up for what's right!

HOTSPOTS

There's a really "uncool" kid in your class. Even some of the nice kids in your class make fun of him. What do you do when you're with a group of friends and you pass him in the hall?

Someone picked up a copy of tomorrow's math test from the teacher's desk. Kids are passing it around at recess. A friends says, "C'mon—everybody's cheating on this test. If you don't, you'll flunk."

One of your good friends starts telling nasty jokes and swearing all the time. What do you do when she asks, "Why don't you ever laugh at my jokes?"

You walked to a nearby mall with a group of friends. You're supposed to be home by 6 o'clock, but your friends say, "Let's stay longer. Tell your mom you weren't wearing your watch and you didn't know what time it was."

You're at a sleep over with several friends. After the parents go to bed, you discover that your friends plan to watch an R-rated horror movie that you know your parents wouldn't want you to see.

Riding your bike home from baseball practice, you see two kids scratching the paint on a car. They warn you to keep quiet about it or they'll get you later.

You're building models in your friend's garage. He holds up a spray can and says, "I've heard that just a few whiffs of this stuff make you feel really cool. Let's try it. It can't be that bad if they sell it in the store."

It's the day before summer vacation. Several of your friends plan to cut class after lunch. They say, "You've gotta cut class too, or you'll ruin it for everybody. C'mon—don't be a nerd."

The Turnaround Project

LESSON AIM

To help kids understand that ★ God wants us to obey him.

OBJECTIVES

Kids or families will

✓ experience frustration when a teammate doesn't follow instructions,
✓ learn about Jonah's struggle to obey,
✓ identify times it's difficult for them to obey, and
✓ commit to obeying God.

YOU'LL NEED

❏ a marker
❏ 2 blindfolds
❏ a large box fan
❏ a spray bottle filled with water
❏ a medium-sized ball
❏ Bibles
❏ paper
❏ pencils
❏ chalkboard and chalk or newsprint and markers
❏ scissors
❏ glue sticks or transparent tape
❏ photocopies of the "Tumbling Pyramids" handout (p. 104)
❏ a bag of small treats*
*Always check for allergies before serving snacks.

BIBLE BASIS

Jonah 1:1–4:11

As you prepare for this lesson, treat yourself to a quick read of the four short chapters that constitute the book of Jonah. Adventure on the high seas—what a plot! Jonah went

all-in-one
SUNDAY
SCHOOL

to great lengths to avoid God's assignment, but God went to greater lengths to reel in the reluctant prophet. Jonah's objections to preaching in Nineveh were not without basis. For the Jews, encouraging the people of Nineveh to find and follow God could almost be considered a breach of national security. Nineveh's military strength posed a constant threat to God's people. Even though Israel's borders were fairly strong and secure in Jonah's time, most Jews viewed God's potential destruction of an enemy city as a positive thing. The Jews (and Jonah himself) seemed to glory in their "favored nation" status with God and cared little for what happened to people outside their borders.

When God told Jonah to go preach repentance to his enemies, Jonah chose to cut and run. Three days in solitary confinement (you can't really count the fish as a companion) helped Jonah adjust his attitude. When the fish spewed the indigestible little prophet out onto the sand, Jonah followed through on God's command. But Jonah was anything but overjoyed when the people of Nineveh reacted with sackcloth, fasting, and prayers of repentance. As Jonah pouted outside the city, God shook him by the shoulders a second time. "Don't you get it, Jonah? I love these people!" The account ends as God makes this point, but we don't know Jonah's final reaction. We can at least give Jonah credit for obedient actions if not altogether obedient attitudes. (Before I shake my finger at Jonah, I think I'll go see what I can do about this log in my own eye.)

John 15:10-11

Jesus knew the cost of obedience. Yet, just before his death, Jesus promised his followers that obedience would result in God's loving presence and the "fullest possible joy."

UNDERSTANDING YOUR KIDS

I wanna do what I wanna do when I wanna do it. Children seem to evidence that attitude within a day or two of exiting the womb, if not before. In children's defense, they do spend most of their early years living out other people's agendas. The frustration of very young children may spill over into tears and tantrums; as kids grow older, we see a range of behaviors from grudging cooperation to full-fledged rebellion.

Children can't wait to grow up—to be the boss. Most have the mistaken impression that adults always get to do exactly what they want to do. Ha! Use this lesson with an intergenerational class to help children see that adults—and famous Bible characters—sometimes struggle with obeying God's commands. They'll also discover that God doesn't give up on us but keeps drawing us back into the circle of his love.

ATTENTION GRABBER

The Tail of the Whale

As people arrive, form teams by using a marker to put a fish mark on the first person's hand and a heart on the second person's hand. Alternate fish and hearts until everyone's hand is marked. It's not necessary for teams to be equally matched. Have the "Fish" and the "Hearts" form separate groups.

Say: **I need one volunteer from each team to step out of the room and be blindfolded.**

If you have adults in your class, choose adult volunteers. Give each of the volunteers a blindfold. As they step out of the room and blindfold each other, give these instructions to both teams: **Your job is to form yourselves into the shape of a whale. You can do it any way you want—just figure out how to make yourselves into a whale. But leave a space where the whale's tail should be. When your blindfolded team member comes back into the room, you'll tell him or her how to join you and finish up the tail of your whale. When your teammate has joined you and your whale is complete, shout, "This whale has a tail!" The members of the team that finishes first will get a treat.**

As the teams form themselves into whale shapes, step out of the room and make sure the volunteers' blindfolds are tied securely. Tell the Heart volunteer to follow his or her team's directions quickly. Tell the Fish volunteer to wander around the room and ignore his or her teammates' directions.

Bring the volunteers back into the room and tell the teams to begin shouting their directions. Be sure to guard the safety of the blindfolded people. After the Heart volunteer has helped the Hearts complete their whale, call time and hand out treats to the Heart team.

Then say: **Time's up!** Gather everyone around you and ask:

♦ **How did you like this game?** (I didn't, because our volunteer didn't follow our directions; I liked it—we got treats.)

Ask the Fish volunteer:

♦ **Why did you ignore what your teammates said?** (Because you told me to; that's what I was supposed to do.)

Say: **Right. I told you to ignore your teammates' instructions because I wanted us all to see what can happen when one person doesn't obey.** Ask the Fish team:

♦ **What happened when your teammate didn't obey you?** (We lost the game; we didn't get a prize.)

Say: **Because your teammate didn't obey you, you lost the**

Teacher Tip

Save some treats for the "Tumbling Pyramids" activity, later in the lesson.

game and the chance to win a treat. **But to be fair, I'll give you each a treat right now.** Hand out treats to the Fish team.

Say: **No one wants to miss out on something good like a snack. When one person fails to obey, lots of people may end up paying the consequences. That is one reason ★ God wants us to obey him. Our Bible story today is about a man who was determined not to obey God, just as** [name of Fish volunteer] **was determined not to obey** [his or her] **teammates. But what was at stake was much more than a treat. A whole city and the lives of all its people were at stake. Let's get right to our Bible story and see what happens.**

BIBLE STUDY

The Turnaround Prophet (Jonah 1:1–4:11)

Say: **I'd like half of the Hearts to form a boat shape on the left side of the room. The Fish can make a big fish shape again here in the middle.** Make sure the fish and the boat are a few feet apart. **The other half of the Hearts can stand over there by the wall on the right side of the room. You'll be the people of Nineveh. Our volunteer who wouldn't follow directions will be Jonah. Jonah, you stand next to the boat.**

Good! Now we're almost ready to begin our Bible story. But first, let me ask you this:

♦ **How would you feel about going and telling people you don't get along with how much God loves them and wants to forgive them?** (I'd be scared; I might go, but I wouldn't like it too much.)

Say: **Well, God asked Jonah to go and preach in an enemy city. The Jews were afraid of the powerful people in Nineveh, and Jonah didn't want to go there. I'm going to read a poem that tells Jonah's story. As I read, listen carefully and act out your part. Here we go!**

Set a large box fan so it will blow on the "boat." Have a spray bottle full of water ready. Read "The Turnaround Prophet" on the following pages and prompt the actions in the story.

After you've finished reading the story, lead everyone in a big round of applause. Gather everyone around you and ask:

♦ **Why didn't Jonah want to obey God?** (Because he didn't like the people of Nineveh; he didn't want to help his enemies.)

♦ **What might've happened to the people of Nineveh if Jonah hadn't gone there to preach?** (God might've destroyed them; something terrible might have happened to their city.)

♦ **Why did God want Jonah to preach in Nineveh?** (Because God loved those people and didn't want to destroy them; God loves everyone and wants everyone to love him back.)

Say: ★ **God wants us to obey him. Because Jonah obeyed, the whole city of Nineveh believed in God!**

THE TURNAROUND PROPHET

(based on Jonah 1:1–4:11)

God talked to Jonah
And let him know one day
To head on out to Nineveh
And go right away!

Though Jonah wasn't friendly
With the people over there,
God wanted him to tell them
To watch and beware!

(Cue the people of Nineveh to look mean and nasty.)
Evil filled their nights,
And bad things filled their days.
God wanted him to warn them now
To change their ways!

Jonah heard quite clearly
The things God had to say,
But the stubborn prophet thought,
"I don't want to obey!

"Those people aren't my friends.
I won't preach there—no way!
Instead of doing what God said,
I think I'll run away."
(Cue Jonah to run and hop into the boat.)

So Jonah packed a bag,
And then he grabbed his coat;
He hurried down to Joppa,
Where he hopped aboard a boat.

Once he got on board the ship,
Jonah went below.
He thought, "No one can find me here;
Not even God will know.

"I think I'll take a little nap;
This spot seems safe and warm."
But little did old Jonah know
That God would send a storm.

The sky turned dark and scary,
And the wind began to blow;
The waves seemed big as mountains
As the boat heaved to and fro.

(Turn the fan on high. Squirt water into the breeze made by the fan.)

The captain said to Jonah,
"Wake up! Wake up, stranger.
Please start praying to your God.
Our ship is in great danger!"

The sailors asked, "Oh, Jonah,
Is this storm your fault?"
"Yes," he said, "here's what to do
To make the storm halt.

"You see, I ran away from God;
I came on board to hide.
But since God sees me, you must
Throw me over the side!"

"We must toss poor Jonah in!
Heave-ho!" cried the crew.
Then they prayed, "Forgive us, Lord,
We want to please you."
(Cue the boat people to gently push Jonah out. Turn off the fan.)

When Jonah hit the water,
He sank down … down … down.
And in the darkness of the sea,
He thought he'd surely drown.

But God was watching Jonah;
To save him was God's wish.
So from the dark depths of the sea
God sent a giant fish.

The fish swam up to Jonah
And with one mighty "Gluup!"
It opened up its giant jaws
And swallowed Jonah up!
(Cue the fish people to "swallow" Jonah.)

"My goodness!" Jonah cried out.
"I'm in a fish—I think.
It's very wet and dark in here
And surely does stink!

(continued)

99

"But can it be God's rescued me?
It seems that I'll survive.
Even though I've disobeyed him,
God's kept me alive!"

Jonah knew just what to do;
He knelt right down to pray.
"Forgive me, God, for I have sinned"
Was all that he could say.

Jonah stayed three days and nights
As the fish's guest.
He prayed, "Lord, when you let me out,
I'll do what you think best."

God told the fish to turn around
And swim toward the land.
Then with one giant hiccup,
Jonah landed on the sand!
*(Cue the fish people to gently push Jonah
    away.)*

He shook himself and looked around
And said, "I'm back! Hooray!
Now I must go to Nineveh,
For I promised I'd obey."

So when he reached that city,
God told him what to say.
"You must leave your sinful ways
And turn to God today."
*(Cue Jonah to walk to Nineveh and preach to
    the people.)*

"God will ruin your city—
He's already set the date.
So pray and tell God you're sorry
Before it's too late!"

The people listened to Jonah.
They knew what he said was true.
They cried and prayed all day long
And even skipped dinner, too!
*(Cue the people of Nineveh to kneel and
    pray.)*

The Ninevites believed in God.
They knew they had been wrong.
They started obeying what God said—
It didn't take them long.

So God forgave the people
For the bad things they had done.
Then the whole town was happy—
All, that is, but one.

It was Jonah who was angry.
He could not understand
Why God would forgive the people
Of such an evil land.

Sitting by a shady vine,
Jonah began to pout.
"Why would God forgive those folks?
I just can't figure it out."
(Cue Jonah to sit and pout.)

The very next day, God sent a worm
To eat away Jonah's vine.
Then Jonah cried, "Why did you take that
    away?
It was shady! It was mine!"

God spoke again to Jonah
And said, "Listen to what I say.
You care a lot for your shady vine
Though I made it in only a day.

"Well, I care for the people of Nineveh,
Just as I care for you.
If I forgave you for your sins,
I can forgive them, too."

There's a lesson to be learned here,
So remember as long as you live
That God always loves us, in spite of our
    sins,
And that when we ask, he'll forgive.

Excerpted from Group's *Hands-On Bible Curriculum*™ for Pre-K & K,
copyright © 1995 Group Publishing, Inc., 1515 Cascade Ave., Loveland, CO 80538.

LIFE APPLICATION

I Hate It When...

Draw a frowny face on a medium-sized ball. Ask:

♦ **Have you ever felt like Jonah—when you knew what was right and what you should do but you really didn't want to do it?** Allow children to respond.

♦ **Why do we get ornery and stubborn?** (Because we're not perfect; because there are other things we'd rather do; sometimes we don't feel like doing what we're told.)

♦ **What was the last thing you had to do that you really didn't want to do?** (Clean my room; help with the dishes; mow the lawn.)

Have everyone stand in a circle. Hold up the ball and say: **This frowny-faced ball stands for things that we really don't want to do. When the ball is tossed to you, finish this sentence: "I hate it when..." For instance, you might say, "I hate it when I have to go to bed early" or "I hate it when I have to pay my income tax." Everybody ready?**

Begin by finishing the sentence yourself; then toss the ball to someone else. Encourage people to toss the ball to those who haven't had it yet.

After everyone has had a turn, set the ball out of sight. Ask:

♦ **Do you think anyone in the whole world gets to do what he or she wants to do most of the time? Explain.** (No, most people have to work or go to school, and they don't have much time for anything else; yes, maybe some rich people get to do what they want to do.)

♦ **Do you think doing what you want to do all the time would make you happy? Why or why not?** (Yes, that would be awesome; no, I'd probably get bored.)

Say: **Let's find out what Jesus said about obeying God. We'll also find out what really makes people happy.**

Form groups of four. Give each group a kid-friendly Bible, paper, and a pencil. Have groups choose two readers, a reporter, and an encourager. Write these Scripture references on a chalkboard or newsprint: "John 14:15-16" and "John 15:10-11." Instruct the readers to read the passages aloud to their groups. Then read these questions one at a time, allowing discussion time between each question:

♦ **Who can name a time Jesus obeyed God even though it was hard?** (When Jesus died on the cross; when Jesus took our sins.)

♦ **How does God help us obey him?** (He sends us a "Helper"; he gives us his love.)

♦ **According to Jesus, what brings joy?** (Being in God's love; obeying God and feeling his love.)

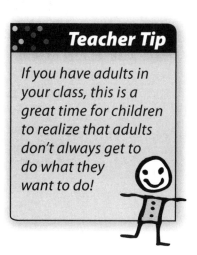

Teacher Tip

If you have adults in your class, this is a great time for children to realize that adults don't always get to do what they want to do!

101

♦ **Jesus promises us wonderful joy if we obey his commands. What are some of Jesus' commands to us?** (To love and obey God; to love each other; to forgive people.)

Call the groups together and invite the reporters to share what they learned from the Scripture passages and from their discussions.

Then say: **God made us, and he knows how hard it can be for us to obey. That's one reason God gives us a Helper—the Holy Spirit. The Holy Spirit reminds us of what God wants us to do, and then gives us the strength to do it. Let's see what good and bad things can happen when we choose to obey and disobey.**

COMMITMENT

Tumbling Pyramids

Set out scissors, glue sticks or transparent tape, and copies of the "Maybe, Maybe Not" section of the "Tumbling Pyramids" handout. Have kids cut on the solid lines, fold on the dotted lines, and fold the handout into a pyramid shape.

When everyone has a completed pyramid, have kids line up across one end of the room facing you. Hold up a bag that contains treats. Say: **We're going to play a game similar to Mother, May I? When I call out a command, toss your pyramids in the air. You'll do whatever it says on the side of the pyramid that lands facing you. As soon as you reach me, you can have one of the treats in this bag. Ready? Here we go!**

Give a series of commands similar to these:
♦ **Shake hands with two people.**
♦ **Sing "Happy Birthday" as fast as you can.**
♦ **Smile and take a bow.**
♦ **Spin around three times.**
♦ **Pinch your nose and say, "I'm a very nice person."**
♦ **Pat yourself on the head.**
♦ **Touch your toes.**
♦ **Make a funny face.**
♦ **Croak like a frog.**
♦ **Do three shoulder rolls.**
♦ **Touch your nose.**

As you give commands, kids will be moving forward or back, depending on how their pyramids land. As kids reach you, give them treats and have them sit and watch the rest of the kids play. Stop the game before they lose interest; then gather everyone in a circle.

Say: **Since some of you had trouble obeying, and since I'm such a nice person, I'll give you a treat anyway.** Ask:
♦ **Why did some of you disobey so often?** (Because of the

way the pyramids landed.)

 ♦ **Why do people disobey in real life?** (They want to do things their way; they don't want to be told what to do.)

 ♦ **What were the consequences of disobeying?** (It took longer to get a treat; it was frustrating.)

 ♦ **What are the consequences when people disobey in real life?** (They sin and mess up their lives; bad things might happen to them.)

 ♦ **What does God want us to do after we've disobeyed?** (Say we're sorry; ask forgiveness and then start obeying.)

 Say: **I have another pyramid for you to make. This pyramid shows how to obey God.**

 Distribute the "Way to Obey" section of the "Tumbling Pyramids" handout and have kids assemble it as before. As kids work on their pyramids, ask:

 ♦ **What's one way you can listen to God this week?** (Stop and check in with God several times a day; listen to God when I get up in the morning.)

 ♦ **What's one way you can make a commitment to obey God this week?** (I can say, "God, I want to obey you"; I can put God first and put things I want to do second.)

 ♦ **Why is it important to pray for God's help?** (He can give us the power to obey; God can make us brave because we know he's with us.)

 ♦ **When do you know it's time to take action?** (When God gives me an opportunity; when God lets me know.)

 Say: **When you get home, you might use a needle and thread to poke through the top of your "Way to Obey" pyramid and make a hanger. Hang it somewhere as a reminder that ★ God wants us to obey him. And remember, Jesus says that when we obey God, our joy will be full!**

CLOSING

Ready to Obey

 Close with a prayer similar to this one: **Dear Lord, thank you for giving us opportunities to live for you and serve you. Help us listen to you every day and help us be ready to obey. Thank you for the joy that comes from obeying you. In Jesus' name, amen.**

Tumbling Pyramids

Cut out the pyramids on the solid lines and then crease them on the dotted lines.
Fold them into pyramid shapes, and secure them with tape or glue.

Maybe, Maybe Not

Way to Obey

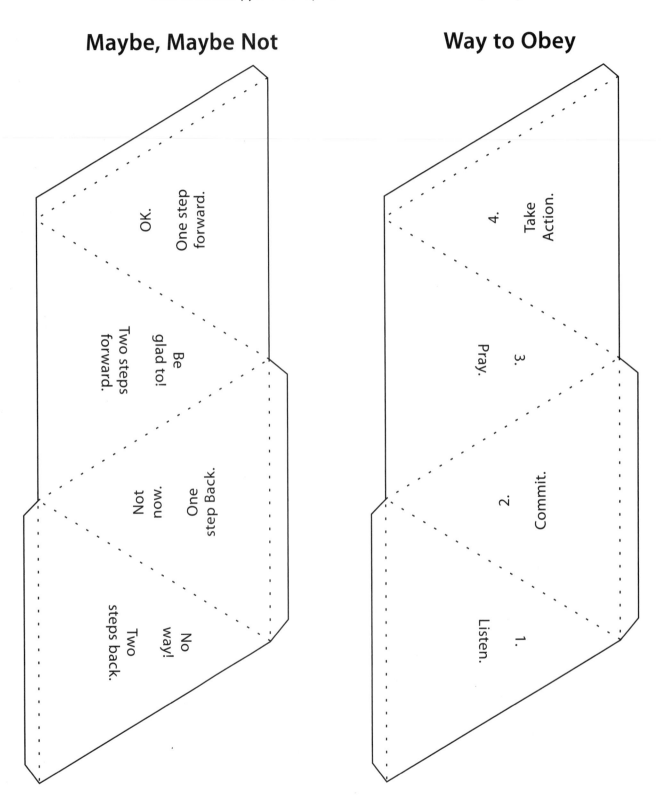

11

LESSON AIM

To help kids realize ★ God wants us to tell the truth.

OBJECTIVES

Kids or families will

✓ participate in creating a silly story,
✓ explore a scriptural example of honesty,
✓ role play telling the truth in difficult situations, and
✓ ask God for help in being honest.

YOU'LL NEED

❏ pen
❏ 2 crowns
❏ 3 bathrobes or bedsheets
❏ false beards and wigs
❏ Bibles
❏ photocopies of the skit "To War or Not to War?" (p. 109)
❏ a long piece of rope or clothesline
❏ a photocopy of the "Tell the Truth" handout (p. 112)
❏ scissors

BIBLE BASIS

2 Chronicles 18:3-34

This story happens during the period of the divided kingdom. Jehoshaphat, king of Judah, was a godly man. But Ahab, king of Israel, made a habit of defying and mocking God. Ahab kept a flock of false prophets around him. Their main purpose in life was keeping the king happy. Micaiah, the one prophet who was in touch with God, had gained himself a poor reputation with Ahab because he insisted on telling the truth. In this story, Micaiah tells the truth even when he knows the king will throw him in prison.

all-in-one
SUNDAY
SCHOOL

In our society, people often do and say "whatever works," rather than whatever is honest. Our challenge is to be as honest, in touch with God, and willing to take a stand as Micaiah was.

John 8:31-32

When Jesus says, "The truth will set you free," he's talking primarily about the freedom that comes from a relationship with God. Once we're free from sin, we're also free to tell the truth, under any and all circumstances.

UNDERSTANDING YOUR KIDS

Even kids from wonderful Christian homes seem to learn to lie just about as soon as they learn to talk. There is something deceitful in human nature that causes us to want to cover our tracks. Honest living is an ongoing challenge for all Christians, kids and adults alike. The key thing to teach kids is God will forgive us for wrongdoing if we're honest about it. Any temporary reprieve gained by dishonest behavior will quickly pass; the loss of integrity is a far greater consequence to pay in the end.

Younger kids can learn that it's okay to tell the truth—if their honest confessions of faults and errors are met with forgiveness and a chance to make a fresh start.

Older kids have mastered the half-truth or "white lie." They need to see that God calls us to perfect integrity and that it's better to live with the consequences of telling the truth than with a murky conscience.

ATTENTION GRABBER

Sunday Sillies

Say: **You've heard of the Sunday funnies in the newspaper. Today we're going to start out with the Sunday Sillies.**

Have kids form three groups, with an adult or older child in each group. Take turns asking the three groups for the words you need to fill in the story Sunday Sillies on the next page.

Say: **I'll ask your groups to give me different kinds of words or names. When it's your group's turn, make a huddle and then call out the word you decide on. When we've filled in all the blanks, I'll read you our Sunday Sillies.** Jot kids' words down in the blanks of the Sunday Sillies story, and then read the story, inserting the kids' words as you read.

After you've read the completed story to the class, ask:

♦ **What's so funny about this story?** (The words don't really fit; it sounds weird.)

♦ **What do we call it when we make up things that aren't true?** (Lying.)

♦ **How is the Sunday Sillies like lying?** (We're just making it up as we go along; it's not really true.)

♦ **How is it different from lying?** (We followed your instructions; we're not doing it to be dishonest.)

♦ **How is copying someone else's paper like lying?** (We're pretending to know something we don't really know.)

♦ **When are people tempted to lie?** (To keep out of trouble.)

Say: **It's fun to make up stories. But in real life, ★ God wants us to tell the truth—even when it's hard. Today we're going to learn about a man in the Bible who did just that.**

BIBLE STUDY

Truth or Consequences (2 Chronicles 18:3-34)

Explain that today's Bible study is in the form of a skit, and everyone gets to take part. If you've invited adults for an intergenerational class, ask three men to take the parts of Ahab, Jehoshaphat and Micaiah. Have kids take the parts of the narrator and the messenger. Tell the rest of the class to say "ooo!" when you point at them.

Have your characters put on the costume items you brought—crowns, bathrobes or bedsheets, beards and wigs.

You may choose to read the narrative directly from the Bible, signaling characters to read as their lines come up. Or

SUNDAY SILLIES

_____ didn't like _____. In fact, it was her most _____ subject.
(girl's name)   (subject in school)   (adjective)

So, she never studied or even did her _____. At the end of the quarter, she
                                        (thing)

was getting a very bad _____.
                        (thing)

"Oh no," she _____. "I'll get a really _____ grade in this subject. What am I
              (past tense of verb)   (adjective)

going to _____?"
          (verb)

On the day of the final test, she was feeling _____. Suddenly she had a/an
                                               (adjective)

_____ idea. _____ was sitting right beside her. He was a/an
(adjective)   (boy's name)

_____ student. She could see his paper _____.
(adjective)   (adverb)

"I'll _____ his paper," she thought. "Then I'll be sure to get a _____ grade.
        (verb)   (adjective)

Suddenly the teacher's shadow _____ across her desk. The teacher snatched
                               (past tense of verb)

up the test paper and _____ it into the _____. _____
                       (past tense of verb)   (thing)   (same girl's name)

knew she was in big _____.
                     (thing)

TO WAR OR NOT TO WAR?

NARRATOR: We're about to witness a meeting between two great kings. *(Signal kids to "ooo!")* Jehoshaphat is the king of Judah. He's a good man who tries his best to follow God. Ahab is the king of Israel. He's a wicked man who does what he pleases and ignores God's laws.

AHAB: Jehoshaphat, great to see you, ol' buddy ol' pal. Doesn't this look like great weather for a war? What d'ya say we get our armies together and go attack Ramoth in Gilead? We could wipe it out in no time and add a few juicy items to our royal treasuries. How about it?

JEHOSHAPHAT: Well sure, I always like to help out a neighbor. But don't you think we ought to check with God about this? I mean, war is serious stuff.

AHAB: Okay, okay. I figured you'd say something like that. *(Shouts)* Call the prophets together!

NARRATOR: Suddenly, 400 prophets appeared on the scene. *(Signal kids to "ooo!")* "Go to war!" they all shouted. "God will give you success." But Jehoshaphat wasn't convinced.

JEHOSHAPHAT: Uh, not to be rude, but don't you have any real prophets?

AHAB: I was afraid you'd ask that. Yes, we have a real prophet. His name is Micaiah. But he always prophesies bad things for me. I can't stand the guy! *(Signal kids to "ooo!")*

JEHOSHAPHAT: You really shouldn't talk that way about the Lord's prophet.

AHAB: Yeah, yeah, I know. Okay, somebody go get Mr. Bad News.

NARRATOR: The king sent a messenger to get Micaiah.

MESSENGER: Look, Micaiah, there are 400 other prophets there, and they're all saying, "Go to war." Give yourself a break! Go along with them and tell the king what he wants to hear.

MICAIAH: I can only say what God tells me to say.

MESSENGER: This could get nasty. *(Signal kids to "ooo!")*

AHAB: Oh, there you are, Micaiah. Nice of you to drop in. Well, what's the word? Should we go to war or not?

MICAIAH: *(Insincerely)* Sure, go ahead. You're bound to win.

AHAB: *(Storming)* Quit clowning around. What are you really thinking?

MICAIAH: *(Looking upward)* I see your armies scattered across the hillside. Their leader is dead. *(Signal kids to "ooo!")*

AHAB: I knew it. Didn't I tell you he never says anything good about me?

NARRATOR: Micaiah's truthful prophecy made the other prophets so mad, one of them came and slapped Micaiah in the face. *(Signal kids to "ooo!")* And Ahab was so mad, he slapped Micaiah in prison and gave him only bread and water. *(Signal kids to "ooo!")*

AHAB: Forget Mr. Bad News. Let's go to war anyway.

NARRATOR: So Ahab and Jehoshaphat and their armies attacked. Just to play it safe, Ahab dressed like a common soldier. But an arrow went right between the sections of his armor, and the wicked king of Israel died that very day. *(Signal kids to "ooo!")*

use photocopies of "To War or Not to War?" in this lesson, a version of the story in skit format.

After the skit, have everyone give the characters a round of applause.

Ask:

♦ **Tell whether you think it was easy or hard for Micaiah to tell the truth.** (Hard, because he knew he could get in trouble with the king; easy, because he knew God would protect him.)

♦ **Why did Micaiah choose to tell the truth when so many people were against him and he knew he would get in trouble?** (He wanted to obey God; he knew God would be on his side no matter what happened.)

♦ **Tell about a situation where it took a lot of courage to tell the truth.** Answers will vary. If you have adults in the class, children will be especially excited to hear about struggles their parents or grandparents had in telling the truth when they were younger.

LIFE APPLICATION

Made Free

Hold up the rope or clothesline. Have everyone stand in a circle.

Say: **I want each of you to think about one time you were not perfectly honest. You don't have to say it out loud—just think about it. Then wrap the rope around yourself one time and pass it on to the next person.**

Coach the wrapping process so that everyone ends up wound snugly, but not too tightly, together.

Make sure you're the last person to wrap up. Then ask:

♦ **How does it feel to be all wrapped up like this?** (Trapped; scary.)

♦ **How is this like what happens when we tell a lie?** (Sooner or later we'll get caught; we get trapped in a web of lies to cover up the first one.)

♦ **What can set us free?** (God's forgiveness sets us free.)

Say: **Jesus told his disciples: "If you continue to obey my teaching, you are truly my followers. Then you will know the truth, and the truth will make you free." Jesus wants us to accept the forgiveness he offers and then live honestly before God and before men.** ★ **God wants us to tell the truth.**

If you've never asked forgiveness for a dishonest act, this would be a good time to do it. Then, as you unwind yourselves, say Jesus' words, "The truth will make you free."

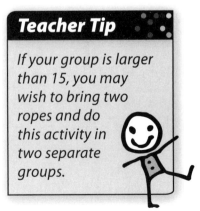

Teacher Tip

If your group is larger than 15, you may wish to bring two ropes and do this activity in two separate groups.

COMMITMENT

To Tell the Truth

After everyone has unwound themselves, say:

★ **God wants us to tell the truth. Let's practice telling the truth by role playing some difficult truth-telling situations.**

Form four groups. Give each group one of the role-plays from the "Tell the Truth" handout. Give groups a few minutes to plan their role-plays. Then have them take turns performing.

After each role-play, ask why it was best to tell the truth in that situation. Encourage kids to tell what might happen if the character tried to hide what really happened.

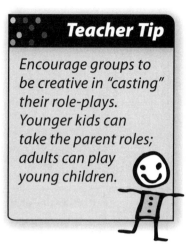

Teacher Tip

Encourage groups to be creative in "casting" their role-plays. Younger kids can take the parent roles; adults can play young children.

CLOSING

Prayer for Courage

Close with prayer, asking God for the courage to be honest even when it's difficult.

As kids leave, have them shake hands with and say to six people, "The truth will make you free."

TELL THE TRUTH

Photocopy and cut apart these truth-telling situations.

Jesus expects us to be honest, even when it's hard. Role play ways to tell the truth in this situation.

A Piece of Cake

There was one piece of cake left. It was supposed to be your brother's. But you were really hungry, and you ate it. Now your brother is screaming that his cake is gone.

Jesus expects us to be honest, even when it's hard. Role play ways to tell the truth in this situation.

An Important Delivery

Your dad was expecting an important delivery from his office. You were supposed to stay home and sign for the delivery. You forgot and went out to play catch with your friends. You remember just as your dad is pulling into the driveway.

Jesus expects us to be honest, even when it's hard. Role play ways to tell the truth in this situation.

An Artful Answer

Your friend wants to enter a picture in an art show. He asks you what you think of it. You think you've seen him draw other pictures that are a lot better.

Jesus expects us to be honest, even when it's hard. Role play ways to tell the truth in this situation.

The Stain

You're having a fight with your sister when your mom isn't home. You get really mad and throw a pillow at her. The pillow knocks her glass of red Kool-Aid onto the carpet. Your mom comes home and finds the stain.

LESSON AIM

To help kids believe that ★ we can trust God when life is unfair.

OBJECTIVES

Kids will

- ✓ discuss reactions to an unfair situation,
- ✓ discover how God worked to protect his people in an unfair situation, and
- ✓ commit to trusting God when they can't understand or see the outcome.

YOU'LL NEED

- ❏ small prizes
- ❏ a blindfold
- ❏ Bibles
- ❏ photocopies of the "Mystery Mosaic" handout (p. 120)
- ❏ crayons

BIBLE BASIS

Esther 1:9–8:12

Talk about spies and international intrigue! The book of Esther contains one of the most exciting stories in the Bible. A wicked prime minister plots the downfall of the Jews, but God comes to the rescue in response to the pleas of a beautiful, obedient queen and her people.

We, in our simple human wisdom, would like to predict God would always bring down the bad guys and rescue the faithful, as happens in the book of Esther. But God's ways are higher than ours, and there are times he allows the righteous to suffer. The bottom line for this lesson is things don't always turn out "fair," but we can trust God to care for us and work out his plans in the end.

all-in-one
SUNDAY
SCHOOL

Psalm 37:1-3

Our society teaches the outcome is everything. The end justifies the means. This psalm directly contradicts that modern philosophy. Our task is simply to trust in the Lord and do good. We can, and should, leave the results with him.

UNDERSTANDING YOUR KIDS

Kids have a tremendously strong sense of justice. Everybody should get the same number of cookies. If I'm nice to you, you should be nice to me. Kids who play fair should win. If we're caught fighting, my punishment should be no worse than yours.

Younger kids trust parents, teachers and other authority figures to legislate fairness in their lives. And they get very upset when justice as they see it isn't done.

Usually by third or fourth grade kids have figured out that life isn't always going to be fair. Parents divorce. Cheaters and bullies sometimes carry the day. Pets and loved ones get sick and die. And trying hard doesn't always mean succeeding. When these things happen, kids can begin to feel that life is out of control.

Kids (and adults!) need to see God is working, even in the midst of devastating circumstances, and his justice will prevail in the end.

☺ The Lesson

ATTENTION GRABBER

Overpowered

Say: **We're going to begin today with some arm-wrestling contests. I'll pair you up for the first match. The winners will each receive one of these.** Show what you brought for prizes.

As you pair kids up, make sure one person in each pair is obviously larger and stronger than the other, so that the outcome of the match will be obvious.

Say "go" and have kids start their matches. Ask all the winners to stand up, and give them each a prize. By now, most of the kids will be objecting and saying, "That's not fair!"

As you distribute prizes to everyone, ask:

♦ **What was unfair about the way I set things up?** (Some people were a lot stronger than their partners; some kids didn't have a chance.)

♦ **How did it feel to have to arm-wrestle someone when you knew you would lose? when you knew you would win?** (I didn't even want to try; I felt sorry for the other person.)

♦ **How were these contests like unfair things that sometimes happen in real life?** (Sometimes teachers or parents make decisions that aren't fair; sometimes all the good guys get on one team at school and we know we'll lose.)

♦ **What's the most unfair thing that ever happened to you?** (I got blamed for something I didn't do at school; I got sick the day we were supposed to go to Disney World; my parents got a divorce.)

Say: **Today we're going to participate in a Bible story that started out with a really unfair situation. Things were so bad, it looked like God's people might be wiped out completely. Let's see what happened as we learn ★ that we can trust God when life is unfair.**

> ### Teacher Tip
>
> *As you set up these obviously unfair contests, kids may protest. Be very positive and encouraging. Say, "I know, but let's just hang in there and see what happens."*

BIBLE STUDY

An Evil Plot (Esther 1:9–8:12)

Practice each of these cues and responses with the class:

♦ **Whenever I say "Esther," the girls fan their hands around their faces and say "ah!"**

♦ **Whenever I say "king," the boys say, "May he live forever!"**

♦ **Whenever I say "Mordecai," press your hands together and say, "A devout Jew."**

♦ **Whenever I say "Haman," everyone boo and hiss.**

THE QUEEN AND THE EVIL PLOT

A mighty king ruled the land of Persia. And a lovely young Jewish girl, Esther, had recently become his queen.

Esther's Uncle Mordecai worked at the palace. One day Mordecai overheard two men plotting to kill the king. He told Queen Esther, who told the king, and the plot was stopped.

Shortly after that, an evil man named Haman became prime minister. He was second in command in the whole kingdom. Haman became so powerful everyone bowed when he walked by—everyone but Mordecai, that is. Haman hated Mordecai because he wouldn't bow down. So Haman thought up an evil plan to get rid of him.

Haman persuaded the king that the Jews were rebellious and dangerous. So the king gave Haman permission to issue a royal decree. On a particular day, all the Jews in Persia were to be killed. And whoever killed them could keep all their money and property. How horrible! How unfair!

When Mordecai heard about this evil plot, he told Queen Esther. "You must go plead with the king, or our people will be destroyed," he said.

The queen was frightened. She could be killed for entering the royal throne room without permission. So Queen Esther told Mordecai, "Gather all the Jews in the city to fast for three days. Don't eat anything!"

Three days later Queen Esther put on her royal robes and entered the throne room. The king welcomed her—she was safe. The Lord had answered the people's prayers. The queen invited the king and Haman to a special banquet that evening.

At the banquet, the king asked: "What is your request? Tell me, and I will grant it." But the queen only smiled and invited the two men to another banquet the next evening.

Haman was proud to be honored at a special banquet given by the queen. And he looked forward to getting rid of Mordecai, the one person who would not bow to him. "Why not get rid of that pesky Jew right away?" his wife suggested. "You can ask permission in the morning to hang him and then go on your way to the queen's banquet." Haman liked the idea, and he immediately had a tall gallows built for hanging Mordecai.

But the Lord had different plans. That night the king couldn't sleep. So he had his servants read to him from the records of the kingdom. They read about the time Mordecai had saved the king's life. "I must honor this man," the king said.

The next morning, <u>Haman</u> arrived to ask permission to hang <u>Mordecai</u>. But before he could speak, the <u>king</u> asked him, "What should I do to honor a man who truly pleases me?"

<u>Haman</u> thought the honor would be for himself. "Oh, Sire, I would put royal robes on him and have someone lead him through the streets on your own horse, shouting, 'This is the way the <u>king</u> honors those who truly please him!'" "Excellent!" the <u>king</u> replied. "Go find <u>Mordecai</u> and do for him just what you've described."

<u>Haman</u> couldn't believe his ears, but he obeyed and led <u>Mordecai</u> through the streets of the city in royal splendor. Then he hurried to the queen's banquet.

"Tell us why you've invited us here," said the <u>king</u>. "What is your wish? I will grant it, even if it is half my kingdom!"

Queen <u>Esther</u> replied, "Please, Your Majesty, save my life and the lives of my people. There is an evil plot against us!"

"Who would dare harm you?" the <u>king</u> demanded.

"He would!" replied Queen <u>Esther</u>, pointing at <u>Haman</u> who had turned pale with fright.

One of the servants came forward and said: "Your Majesty, this man has just had a tall gallows built. He was planning to hang <u>Mordecai</u> on it—the very same man who saved your life!"

"Hang <u>Haman</u> on his own gallows!" the <u>king</u> ordered. And so they did.

Soon afterward, <u>Mordecai</u> became the new prime minister. He got permission to issue a royal decree telling the Jews to defend themselves on the day they were to be killed. The <u>Lord</u> didn't let his people down. Instead of being destroyed, they became stronger than ever.

♦ Whenever I say "Lord," respond by saying "God Almighty!"

Then say: **Ready? Here we go with the story, "The Queen and the Evil Plot."**

Read aloud "The Queen and the Evil Plot" story. Pause after each underlined word to let kids do their actions.

After the story, ask:

♦ **How would you have felt if you had been one of the Jews who was going to be killed?** (Angry; scared.)

♦ **Instead of getting angry or frustrated at God, what did Mordecai and Esther do?** (They fasted and got other people to fast with them; they trusted God to help them; they came up with a wise plan.)

117

◆ **How do you think God wants us to respond when unfair things happen in our lives?** (He wants us to pray and trust him; to act wisely.)

Say: ★ **We can trust God when life is unfair. God cares about us and will always work things out for the best.**

LIFE APPLICATION

Why Worry?

Say: **God wants us to ★ trust him when life is unfair and when we face scary situations—just like Esther and Mordecai did. Let's see what that kind of trust feels like.**

If you have more than 15 kids, you may want to do this activity in groups of 10 kids to save time. Have kids form pairs. Pair older kids with younger ones. Send one pair out of the room. Have the other pairs form an obstacle course with their bodies. They can sit, stand, kneel or create arches.

Blindfold one member of the pair who left the room. Then have the sighted partner lead the blindfolded partner around the obstacle course. Have the partners change roles and go through the course again.

Send another pair out of the room and have the rest of the kids create a different obstacle course. Continue until each person has gone through the obstacle course blindfolded.

Then gather kids in a circle and ask:

◆ **What was it like to go through the obstacle course without being able to see?** (It was scary; it was kind of fun; I didn't want to do it.)

◆ **How important was your partner's help?** (Really important; I'd never make it without a partner.)

◆ **How did it feel to trust your partner?** (I didn't know if I could trust him; I wish she had talked to me more.)

◆ **How is that like trusting God when we don't know how things are going to turn out in our lives?** (We know God is there, but we don't know exactly what he's doing; sometimes we wish we could really see God and have him explain things to us.)

Have kids open their Bibles to Psalm 37:1-3, and have a volunteer read the passage aloud.

Ask:

◆ **What's hard about trusting God when life seems unfair?** (Sometimes it seems like he's not helping us or he doesn't care.)

◆ **How is trusting God like or unlike trusting your partner?** (I have to rely on him when I don't understand what's going on; God won't ever mess up or let me down, but my partner might.)

Teacher Tip

Younger children may be a bit baffled about how to coach their partners. Help them out with a few prompts. For example, ask: "Will you need to hold your partner's hand here? What will you tell your partner to do to get through this part?"

118

COMMITMENT

Just Trust

Give kids each a photocopy of the "Mystery Mosaic" hand-out and a crayon.

Say: **When you solve this mystery, you'll know exactly what God wants you to do the next time you feel like life isn't fair.**

Allow time for kids to color in the spaces with the dots and discover the words "just trust." Encourage kids to keep the secret until everyone has discovered the words. Have older kids help younger kids figure the words out.

Then have kids each use the framed space to draw or write about one unfair situation in their life (or in the world) in which they need to trust God.

CLOSING

God at Work

Bring everyone together and ask volunteers to share what they drew or wrote about. Join hands and close with prayer, asking God to work out things for the best in each of these situations, just as he did for Mordecai and Queen Esther.

MYSTERY

LESSON AIM

To help kids see that ★ when temptation comes, God wants us to walk away!

OBJECTIVES

Kids will

✓ play a game that simulates the excitement of temptation,
✓ learn what happened to Achan when he dabbled in forbidden things,
✓ develop strategies for resisting temptation, and
✓ be reminded of the importance of their relationship with God.

YOU'LL NEED

❏ a bandanna
❏ 1 marble for each child
❏ a table
❏ Bibles
❏ newsprint
❏ marker
❏ tape
❏ photocopies of the "Walk Away!" handout (p. 127)
❏ pencils

BIBLE BASIS

Joshua 6:1–7:26

Fascination with dabbling in forbidden territory goes as far back as Adam and Eve. God's rules were clear. Choosing to ignore those rules even "just this once" changed all of humanity's relationship with God forever.

To God, the clearing of Canaan was serious business. All inhabitants of the towns and countryside were to be killed, right down to the livestock. All valuables were to be brought

to the treasury of the Tabernacle. God wanted his people to be untainted by anything associated with pagan Canaanite religions.

But when an Israelite named Achan caught sight of a beautiful Babylonian robe and a pile of gold and silver, he thought, "Surely it wouldn't matter if I took this stuff just this once ..." Direct disobedience brought serious consequences: a lost battle, and public disgrace and the stoning of Achan's entire family.

God's rules are for real today, just as they were in Achan's time. There's only one thing to do in the face of temptation: Walk away!

1 Corinthians 10:13

Kids tend to think the problems and temptations they face are different from what anybody else faces. But Paul assures us God doesn't allow temptations that millions of others haven't faced, too. And besides that, kids can gain confidence that no temptation is too great to overcome. God promises a way out—and he'll be there to help if we let him.

UNDERSTANDING YOUR KIDS

Kids know all about temptation. It starts with the forbidden dip into the cookie jar and eventually grows to potentially life-threatening proportions as kids are offered drugs and alcohol. It's important for us as adults to see what lies behind kids' desires to overstep safe, established boundaries.

For both younger and older kids the motivation is often curiosity—the desire to know things firsthand rather than accepting the knowledge and warnings of those in authority. Rebellion also plays a part. Kids want to set their own boundaries rather than accept the limitations others set.

In today's "whatever works for you" society, kids need God's boundaries more than ever. They need to understand God isn't some mean old man in the sky; he gave us rules because he loves us. And kids need to see a few moments of excitement dabbling in forbidden zones can bring disastrous results.

 The Lesson

ATTENTION GRABBER

Steal the Jewels

If it's a bright, sunny day, play this game outside on a grassy surface. Have kids stand in a circle about 10 feet across. Choose one person to be "It." Tie up the marbles in a bandanna and put these "jewels" at the feet of whoever's It. If you have more than 20 kids, form multiple circles. You'll need a bandanna and marbles for each circle.

Say: **The object of this game is to steal the jewels. But be careful—if the person who's It touches you, you're frozen until the end of the game. If you manage to steal the jewels and get back to your place in the circle, then you get to be It and a new game starts.**

You can play several rounds of this game because someone usually gets the jewels in just a few seconds. This game works really well with kids of mixed ages because younger kids can dart in and out quickly, and they have the advantage of being smaller targets.

After a few rounds of play, ask:

♦ **What was this game like for you?** (It was exciting and scary; there was the chance I could get the jewels without getting caught.)

♦ **How is playing this game like giving in to temptation?** (We go after the jewels even though we know it's dangerous.)

♦ **How is it different?** (It's just a game—we don't really break any rules or do anything wrong; we're supposed to go after the jewels.)

Say: **Temptation usually involves breaking rules. Or doing something we know we're not supposed to do. Usually there's something we want; we know what the rules are, and we make a choice. ★ When temptation comes, God wants us to walk away. The person we're going to learn about in today's Bible story made a bad choice. Let's see what happened to him.**

Teacher Tip

If kids have trouble stealing the jewels, hint that they can all go for the bandanna at once. Most of the kids will get frozen, but someone is bound to get through.

BIBLE STUDY

Tempted! (Joshua 6:1–7:26)

Say: **After more than 300 years of slavery in Egypt and 40 years of camping in the desert, the Hebrew people are ready for a new home in the land of Canaan. There's just one little problem. There are already people in the land, and** they're not about to move out so God's people can move in. This means war!

The people of Canaan lived in cities with high, strong walls. We're going to make one of those cities right now.

Have kids help you put a table in the center of the room. Put the jewels (still in the bandanna) from the "Steal the Jewels" activity under the center of the table. Then form two groups, with older kids in one group and younger kids in the other. Have the older kids form a city wall by standing around the table in a circle, facing outward.

Say: **We've just built the city of Jericho. Now the rest of you are going to be the army that conquers the city.** Ask:

♦ **How did God tell Joshua to attack Jericho?** Several kids may be familiar with the directions Joshua gave to his army. Review them by having volunteers read aloud Joshua 6:1-8, 14-16 from a kid-friendly Bible.

Say to the younger kids: **Okay, you soldiers have your marching orders. Let's march around Jericho seven times.**

Lead the soldiers in a vigorous march seven times around the "walls." Then lead the soldiers in a shout on the count of three, and cue the walls to collapse.

Have everyone sit on the floor as you continue the story.

Say: **That was a pretty impressive victory! But a problem came up when one of the soldiers didn't follow orders. Joshua told his troops to bring all the treasure out of the city and give it to the priests as an offering to God. So they did—all except for one man named Achan. Achan came up to a house and looked inside.**

Lead kids in peeking under the table.

Say: **There he found treasure—bags of silver and gold and a beautiful robe.**

Open the bandanna and display the marbles that represent the treasure. Ask:

♦ **What was Achan supposed to do with the treasure?** (Bring it to the priests.)

Say: **But he thought: "I could be rich! The priests would never miss this little bit of gold and silver." So he took the treasure and hid it in his tent.**

So Achan became a rich man and lived happily ever after. Right? Wrong! Because Achan gave in to temptation, terrible things happened. The Hebrews lost their next battle, and God showed Joshua that Achan was to blame. So to remove the sin from the Hebrew people, Achan and his whole family were killed. Ask:

♦ **Why did this story have such a sad ending?** (Because Achan gave in to temptation.)

♦ **How do you think Achan felt after he got caught?** (Guilty; scared; sad.)

♦ **Do you think Achan would've felt that way even if he hadn't been caught? Why or why not?** (Yes, he still would've felt guilty and scared because he knew he had done something wrong; no, he made a choice to disobey God, so he didn't care what God or anybody else thought.)

Say: **God doesn't usually deal with disobedience today by killing people. But when we disobey him, we're hurting our friendship with him. And it makes him sad. ★When temptation comes, God wants us to walk away.**

LIFE APPLICATION

Temptation Today

Ask:

♦ **How do you think people feel about giving in to temptation, even if they don't get caught?** (Some people don't care about sin; people who don't get caught still feel sad and guilty.)

♦ **What kinds of things tempt kids today?** (Cheating in school; using bad language; talking back to parents and teachers; trying cigarettes or alcohol; watching the wrong kinds of TV shows and movies; taking candy or music from stores.) List kids' answers down one side of a sheet of newsprint taped to a wall.

♦ **What happens when kids give in to temptations like these?** For every temptation on the list, have kids suggest a consequence. Jot answers on the other half of the newsprint.

COMMITMENT

Walking Away

Give kids each a photocopy of the "Walk Away!" handout and a pencil. Have a volunteer read the Bible verse out loud.

Say: ★ **When temptation comes, God wants us to walk away. Let's look at the list we made of things that tempt us. How could we walk away from them?**

Read the items from the list, and have kids tell ways to walk away from each one. Then have kids use the blank space on the handout to draw something that tempts them. Demonstrate how to fold the handout so the tempting thing "disappears."

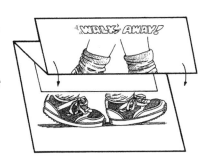

After kids have finished drawing, ask:

♦ **How does walking away from temptation make it disappear?** (The temptation doesn't really disappear, but walking away helps me avoid giving in.)

♦ **How does thinking about temptation make it harder to resist?** (The more I think about something, the more I want it.)

CLOSING

The Greatest Treasure

Give kids each one of the marbles from the "Steal the Jewels" activity.

Say: **Things that tempt us may look good for a while. But there are always consequences to pay if we give in. Take this marble with you today to help you remember God is our greatest treasure, and we don't want to give in to any temptations and destroy our relationship with him. ★ When temptation comes, God wants us to walk away.**

Close with prayer, asking God to help kids walk away from temptations that come into their lives.

WALK AWAY!

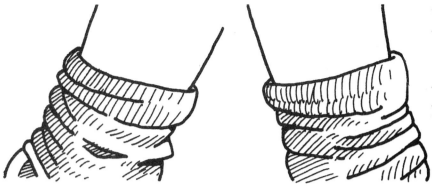

What's your biggest temptation? Draw it in the blank space below. Then fold it out of sight, and remember to walk away the next time you face temptation.

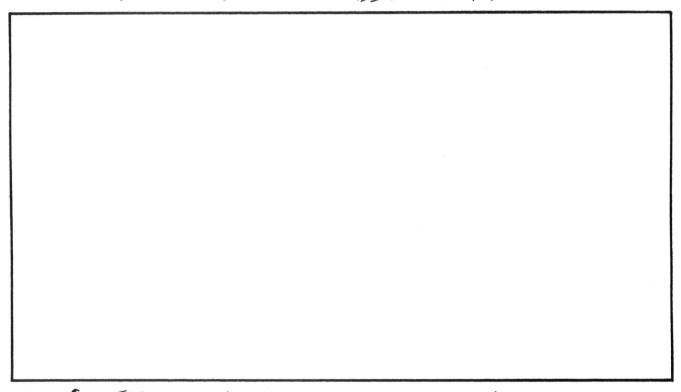

"The temptations in your life are no different from what others experience. And God is faithful. He will not allow the temptation to be more than you can stand. When you are tempted, he will show you a way out so that you can endure" 1 Corinthians 10:13.